THE
MED SCHOOL
SURVIVAL GUIDE

THE
MED SCHOOL
SURVIVAL GUIDE

101 Ways to Make the Challenges of Medical School Seem Like Small Stuff

JENNIFER DANEK, M.D.

THREE RIVERS PRESS / NEW YORK

Published by Three Rivers Press, New York, New York. Member of the Crown Publishing Group.

Random House, Inc. New York, Toronto, London, Sydney, Auckland
www.randomhouse.com

Three Rivers Press is a registered trademark and the
Three Rivers Press colophon is a trademark of Random House, Inc.

Printed in the United States of America

Design by Karen Minster

Library of Congress Cataloging-in-Publication Data

Danek, Jennifer.
The med school survival guide: 101 ways to make the challenges
of medical school seem like small stuff / by Jennifer Danek.
1. Medical students—Psychology.   2. Student adjustment.
3. Medical education—Miscellanea.   I. Title.
[DNLM: 1. Education, Medical.   2. Schools, Medical.
3. Students, Medical—psychology.
W 18 D179m 2000]
R737.D34 2000
610'.71'1—dc21   00–020105

ISBN 0-609-80595-9

10   9   8   7   6   5   4   3   2

First Edition

This book is for my mother and father,
who have given me the most potent medicine of all—
unconditional love.

It is also dedicated to my sisters
Huong and Kyra,
who kept my spirit alive and my integrity intact
throughout medical school. To this day, they continue
to teach me what it means to be a healer.

CONTENTS

"Every potential health-care provider makes the choice as to whether he or she is to be a disease technician or a healer. Jennifer Danek's delightful book provides practical suggestions that can enable larval doctors to keep their souls. Both they and the communities they are entrusted to care for will benefit from the simple and profound wisdom contained in *The Med School Survival Guide*." —DAVID SIMON, M.D.,

Medical Director,
The Chopra Center for Well Being

"Dr. Danek's amazing connection to medicine and humanity is evident on every page. The advice she shares is important to physicians old and new, and actually to all of us, regardless of profession or station in life. Read *The Med School Survival Guide* and Thrive!" —MICHAEL V. DRAKE, M.D.,

Steven P. Shearing Professor of Ophthalmology,
University of California, San Francisco

"*The Med School Survival Guide* is definitely an insider's book. With wit, grace, and great insight, Dr. Danek offers those who struggle to prepare themselves as doctors with wisdom to live fully and well. It is hard to know how any of us survived medical school without it."

—RACHEL NAOMI REMEN, M.D.,
Clinical Professor, School of Medicine,
University of California, San Francisco

ACKNOWLEDGMENTS

I am extremely grateful for the experience of becoming a physician and for those people who have taught me along the way. Caring and compassionate physicians such as Dr. Dan Lowenstein, Dr. Rachel Remen, and Dr. Michael Drake have served as role models and have been a source of inspiration over the years. Innumerable lessons have come from my classmates and patients. It is your wisdom and your stories that I hope to capture in this book.

I would like to extend my appreciation to PJ Dempsey for the opportunity to write this book, and for her continued support of me. A big thank you goes to Kyra Bobinet for the writings and the insight that she contributed. I also recognize Sarah Silbert for her patience and her careful editing, and the many others at Three Rivers Press whose hard work made it possible for this book to be completed.

Most of all I thank God, for all the deepest of understanding comes from this source. Writing this book has been a great blessing for me and I am grateful to be able to share this with others.

INTRODUCTION

From the age of six, I was preparing to become a doctor. Much of my undergraduate years were dedicated to getting into medical school. Finally I was accepted. On the first day of medical school, one of the prominent physicians of the school welcomed the new class. Looking out upon one hundred forty-one excited and innocent faces, he proclaimed, "Today, you are full of humanity. Unfortunately, most of you will spend the next four years losing it."

This wasn't the first time I had heard such admonitions. People always said that medical school was a sacrifice, but somehow I refused to believe it. I thought that I was different, that I could maintain my same lifestyle and simply change my focus of study. I thought that I could stay the same person, only tack an M.D. onto the end of my name. After all, I liked who I was.

That day, for the first time, the reality of being a medical student started to sink in. I listened intently as the physician pleaded with us to remain idealists, to seek meaning beyond exams, and to get help when we needed it. I felt like a soldier getting rallied for the battle. I had the same queasy demented feeling. That's when I knew medical school was going to be intense.

The truth is, medical school will change your life. It will be intense.

You will have to make sacrifices. But it is also an extraordinary honor and privilege to be trained as a doctor. In medical school, you will gain the knowledge to heal the sick and be present with the dying. You will be surrounded by experts in all fields. You will meet the people who will be your lifetime friends. You may even find your future spouse (for whatever reason, the gross anatomy lab seems to be a hot spot).

This book addresses the specific challenges of medical students' lives. Every medical student will confront feelings of self-doubt or stress. All of you will be pressed for time and need to juggle multiple responsibilities. Some of you will suffer depression or other illnesses. It is my deep belief that it is not circumstances but the way in which you react to them that will determine your medical school experience. Every challenge you face can either take you down, or it can elevate you to a higher level.

This book is written for all of you who wish to "remain whole" through a tough and trying process. It is intended to help you realize what an honor it is to be a medical student. It will also help you to counter those forces that would have you forget or distort this honor. It is my hope that when you pick up this book, you will find new ways to keep the faith, to enjoy and learn more, and to stay true to your own integrity.

The goal of this book is not only to help you survive medical school. It is to advance you to the full of your potential—not just in your studies, but in all of your humanity. It is to help you become your highest self and the best doctor you can be.

THE
MED SCHOOL
SURVIVAL GUIDE

1

BEGIN WITH A HEALTHY ATTITUDE

1. REMEMBER WHO YOU ARE

In the first week of medical school, most new students walk around in a state of shock. The collective feeling is "Pinch me, I must be dreaming." Yes, after all of your work, you're here. The biomedical library, the cheap pharmaceutical freebie stethoscope, the greasy hospital food—it's all yours. This reality is hard to accept, but true. You are now training to be a doctor.

Of course you're excited. You're immersed in a new world. You're envisioning "Dr." before your name and salivating over your first white coat. It's a whole new you! Or is it? My advice for everyone at this point is to take it slow. Before jumping into your new identity, take a moment to remember who you are.

Consider medical school a long experiment in understanding yourself. If you don't know yourself coming in—or at least value the question of who you are—you're likely to be swept along by powerful forces that will define it for you. If you have a strong sense of yourself and continue to feed all aspects of your person, then medical school will make you stronger and richer.

On the first day of medical school, write down the things that matter to you. What kind of physician do you want to be? What are the little things that make you happy? What are your goals to accomplish during medical school? Revisit this list from time to time. In the midst of crazy exam schedules, you'll remember just how much you love to write poetry and set time aside for it. At the very least, it will give you some perspective. It will remind you of who you are and why you wanted to become a doctor in the first place.

2. WELCOME CHANGE

When I first started medical school, I was scared to death of change. I knew that medical school would put me through the wringer, and I would emerge on the other end looking, feeling, and acting different. It wasn't a comforting thought. I had heard about and seen many examples of what I didn't want to happen with my life. To me, change was synonymous with loss of self, loss of freedom, loss of youth. Needless to say, with this attitude, I approached medical school with both fists raised, full of doubt and suspicion.

There is a saying "either you change or you die." Most people are not good at accepting either of these conditions. In medical school, however, you are constantly facing both: change and death. You shift from one class to the next, one medical team to the next, and one hospital to the next. People come in your life, and they leave, or they die. Over four years, many of you will transition from being a dependent young student to an adult physician with major responsibilities.

The reality is that change is a good, natural process. And medical school, if you welcome the change, can be an enlightening experience— one that brings greater freedom and a deepening understanding of yourself. I've seen this happen with a lot of my classmates. Once they realized that medical school wasn't going to strip them bare and leave them empty, they began to enjoy the experience and learn from it. They were able to imagine themselves as doctors and take on this responsibility. With this acceptance comes a new level of joy and peace.

Change isn't a choice; how you change is the choice. If you see medical school (and your life) as a process of change, you will feel invigorated by the challenges that await. And rather than resist the losses, you will appreciate how much you have to gain from the process of becoming a doctor.

3. TRUST THE ADMISSIONS COMMITTEE

The first great obstacle in arriving at any medical school is believing that you deserve to be there. Undergraduate training and the admission process is an intensive process designed to weed out and whittle down the masses, so that only the best (or the luckiest) make it. It's only natural to feel a little shocked when you arrive at medical school. Someone else actually believes you could be a doctor—or do they?

In the first year of medical school, most medical students suffer from the admissions-committee-made-a-mistake syndrome. Listening to the Dean's opening remarks, it seemed only a matter of time before I would be pulled aside and told that my name had accidentally escaped the computer's reject list. I was stunned by the brilliant, compassionate people around me, but I failed to realize that I was one of them. Little did I know, everybody else felt the same way.

It's time that you learn to appreciate your own greatness. Trust in the fact that if you make it through the grueling admission process, you are meant to be there. You have the intelligence to master the academic side of medicine, and the attributes to be a competent and compassionate doctor. The admissions committee chose you deliberately. If you don't know what they saw in you that was inspiring, you need to find out.

4. Don't Complain

Attitude is ninety-nine percent of our experience. I am convinced of this. I have classmates who could empty urinals all day and be happy. I also know students who have the best rotations and most caring teachers and still find a reason to complain.

Be wary not to fall into the rut of complaining. It usually starts right after the high of realizing you are in medical school. You begin to understand what it entails, and then the grumbling begins. Medical school is tough, man. How can I function when they only let me have two hours of sleep? Why do we have to learn all these darn enzymes anyway? If this sounds remotely familiar, take heed. Complaining may start off benign, but it can lead to major discontentment and disillusionment.

Here's what you do: Stay away from the complainers. Distance yourself! Secondly, look at the bright side. It sounds trite, but there really is something you can learn by running lab tests here and there for a lazy resident (like, um, humility). Try not to jump the gun in assuming that any situation is catastrophic. Sometimes, things that appear dismal will surprise you. And finally, remember that you have a choice. Nobody is forcing you to do anything.

If you take a positive approach, you'll be amazed at what you find. With the eyes of gratitude, medical school will be more often filled with wonder, rather than angst.

5. Have Fun

In medical school, my fellow students nicknamed me "Happy." It wasn't that I was always happy, but I enjoyed the little things. I liked to begin the day with my favorite scone. I liked to dress up, no matter what the occasion. I liked being outside, so I'd skip class and study in Golden Gate Park. For me, these things were as important as my studies. They were the things that allowed me to be "happy." Without them, I wouldn't be able to maintain anything, especially my studies.

There are two very different types of medical students—those that will have a good time anywhere, and those that, despite their own choices, feel cajoled and unappreciative of any situation. Stay away from the latter. Cynicism is a dangerous attitude, and it will quickly take you down in medical school. Instead, seek out classmates that share a positive outlook.

Some of the most joyful and humorous experiences of my life occurred in the daily activities of medical school. I'm sure my class-mate will always remember that late night in the anatomy lab when he opened his mouth to demonstrate the veins and arteries under his tongue. I was so excited to locate the lingual artery that I pointed it out to my classmates. It wasn't until he screamed in horror that I realized my gloved finger, full of cadaver tissue, was in his mouth! These are the experiences of medical school—the odd, the extreme, and the wonderful—that become a part of your life. To enjoy them in the moment (as did my classmate, who was a good sport) is to be truly living.

6. Give Up Being the Best

Most pre-meds come from an environment in which they excelled above and beyond their peers. Gather these people together and you have a room full of inflated egos. Welcome to medical school. If you wish to maintain your status as the "best," you're going to confront a lot of competition. And you'll still come up short. In this environment, you simply can't be the expert in everything. No matter how good a student you are, someone else will likely know more than you—if not other students, then the intern or resident.

Here's an idea: Give up being the best. I'm not suggesting that you lower your standards. I'm saying that you should set your own priorities and stop comparing yourself to everyone else. It takes a lot of energy to prop up your ego, and eventually it makes you neurotic and unhappy. So let it go. Redirect your time and energy to more efficient learning and a more balanced life. If gross anatomy is your weak point, let your classmate who is the aspiring surgeon stay up all night learning the pelvic vasculature. Then ask him to teach you. Make choices not to cram in an extra two hours of studying the night before the exam if you already know the material. You give up an extra two points on the exam, but you spend that time in a way that is meaningful for you.

The decision to lower your competitive drive is a long-term invest-ment in your well-being. This approach will provide the greatest returns in the end—freeing up your time and your mind, and ultimately being more happy with your life.

7. Remember "This Too Shall Pass"

In medical school (as in life), little things can become big. Two days before your physiology exam, understanding total lung capacity and forced residual volumes may become the most important thing in your life. But is it really?

When you're in the thick of things, remember the adage "This too shall pass." Stretch your vision into infinity, and ask yourself how much will this matter when all is said and done. It helps to remember events in your life that seemed massive at the time, but are hardly even remembered. Think of when you broke up with your first "real love." Even that event, which was likely devastating to you, soon passed and became small in the scheme of things.

I'm not advising that you blow things off or diminish the importance of day-to-day living. Rather, this rule helps you to regain your perspective. Say that you get a macho cowboy-type from Texas as your senior resident. He can even make your life a living hell for six weeks. But guess what? After that, you never have to see him again. A year from now, you'll hardly remember his name. So take it in stride. Let all your obsessive thoughts about showing him up, or telling him off, or bailing yourself out just float right by. When he's got you so aggravated you could just scream, zoom your focus out into the big picture. Remind yourself: "This too shall pass."

8. REFRAIN FROM GOSSIP

Going to medical school is kind of like returning to high school—four years of the same classes, in the same rooms, with the same people. And, of course, gossip. Gossip is an inevitable aspect of a small, closed community. In medical school, it isn't quite as vicious as high school (we call it "small talk"), but it's gossip nonetheless. It means that, within a short period of time, you'll know everything about what's happening with everyone else. News flashes come frequently—the latest on a know-it-all classmate, marital problems of another, a gay professor.

Gossip locks you into one circuit—medical school. After a while, this gets old and dull, and so do we. We may find that we really are interested in some ridiculous detail of someone else's life. That's a telltale sign of impending doom. Get out while you can, before you become a single-minded bore.

Make a commitment to focus on the things that really matter. Resist the urge to speculate about others or speak on issues you don't know are true. Instead, engage in more meaningful conversations and practice listening. In speech (as in life), you get what you give.

9. Develop Your Staying Power

Our biggest enemy in life is not our failures; it's giving up. If you look at the major discoveries of our time, the great advances in science, the most profound social movements—all were preceded by many failures. In the end, however, there was achievement. What distinguishes great people is not their ideas, but rather their ability to persist in the face of obstacles. This is the quality that you will need to nurture above all others in medical school. I call it "staying power."

In medical school, it helps to remember that you're never given anything in life that you can't handle. If a situation causes you discomfort, or mental anguish, or embarassment, it just means that you have something to learn. Perhaps you've done something wrong that you need to make right, or you're holding on to a belief that you need to change. I sincerely believe that the world will teach us what we need to know. With this perspective, I know that the toughest situations are just trying to teach us something. We need to hang in there until we get it.

Medical school is a crash course in developing staying power. You'll be challenged in ways that you never could have imagined. Through the toughest experiences, you'll learn where your limits are and glean the lessons that you need to carry on. It's like my grandmother used to say: What doesn't kill you makes you stronger.

10. Don't Expect Others to Understand

Medical school is a unique experience that is outside the realm of ordinary life for most people. The sheer madness of memorizing lists of microorganisms or staying up nights on end can only be understood by living it. It's like a man trying to comprehend the pain of childbirth. He can empathize and provide comfort, but he can never fully understand what the woman is going through.

Lowering your expectations of other people will surprisingly make things easier and less stressful as you go through this "unique experience." It is natural to want the people who are close to you to understand you, particularly during times of crisis or stress. But if your expectations of them exceed what they are capable of providing, then they fall short in your eyes. This is a source of frustration and disappointment for everyone.

All of us, when we are struggling, have a tendency to be self-centered. When no one is there to hear your med school pains, it can seem like the whole world is letting you down. Your professor doesn't understand how hard you studied for the exam you failed. Your mother is helping your little sister when you call for support. Your best friend wants to talk about some new girl he's dating.

Paradoxically, the less you expect others to respond, the more you appreciate what you receive from those around you. The less that you turn to others for your happiness, the more you learn to create happiness for yourself. Try this approach the next time you feel misunderstood. Instead of feeling angry at someone else, take a positive action to help yourself. Go for a run, pray, or listen to an inspiring song. If you do this, you'll find that you are your own best friend.

11. Compose a List of Thirty Things You Want to Do Before You Die

In a moment when you are feeling clear and inspired, write a list of thirty things you want to do before you die. Don't place any limits on yourself. You'll be surprised at what flows from you. They may be simple, like having children or tending a garden. Or they may be goals that you set for yourself—graduating from medical school or becoming an orthopedic surgeon. There are bound to be a few odd ones (I won't divulge mine) that seem farfetched or implausible. Put them down anyway. Medical school focuses your attention in one place; this exercise does the opposite. It helps you to broaden your attention to all the possibilities for your life. I am always surprised when I revisit my list how relevant it still is to who I am today. I still want to learn Hindi and spend a month on a canoe. And I'm shocked that I could foresee the things I would later do—writing a book, learning a unique dance form, teaching children.

If you ask people who have tackled great feats in their life, it began by believing that it might be able to happen. Once I saw Oprah speak. She talked about how her grandmother would boil clothes in the backyard, saying "Girl, you better learn how to do this because one day it will be you out here." Right then, she thought to herself, "Oh no, I won't, Grandma." Instead, she left Mississippi, with dreams of using her "talking" skills. When she was turned down for jobs, she would say, "You watch me, one day I'm going to be famous."

Chances are you'll die with most of your list uncompleted. That's not the point. The point is to start dreaming. The point is to never abandon your dreams—and to keep coming up with new ones. No matter what they are, all is possible.

12. Understand that Others Feel the Same Way

Many of us suffer from the syndrome of believing "the grass is greener on the other side." We feel like everyone else has it easy. We see all their talent, their successes, and their opportunities. From this vantage point, it seems that everyone else has carefree, happy lives. Everyone, except us.

The truth is, no matter what you're feeling—stressed out, lonely, confused—you're not alone. The experience of medical school brings out feelings that are universal. You feel you may not be cut out for medicine. You can't keep up. You're overwhelmed. It hits each person at different times and to different degrees, but everyone goes through it.

In my med school class, I remember one person who seemed to do everything with perfect ease. He was always meticulously prepared, knew all the answers, and got the highest scores. Often, I wished that I had it as easy as he did. Then one day in our third year, he told me how he felt completely incompetent. Every exam he was terrified of failing, and he felt that no matter how much he studied he never knew enough. All this time, I had envied him, only to realize that inside, he had many of the same feelings I had.

Remind yourself from time to time that you are not alone. Think of this the next time you are in class and are embarrassed to ask a question. Tell yourself that if you're confused about a certain point, other people are feeling the same way and would appreciate you speaking up. If you're feeling overwhelmed or depressed, you don't have to be ashamed to ask your professor or a counselor for help. Dozens of other people have been through the same thing.

13. Remember—It's Your Choice

Despite what you may think of the demands of medical school, your ability to choose is never taken away from you. Think of this the next time that you are inclined to grumble or complain. What choice do you have?

One choice you have made is to become a doctor. This choice is not laid in stone. Take the approach that each day you will decide again whether to continue medical school or not. Try it. It's a simple shift in thought, but it radically changes the way you look at your world. Hopefully, despite little frustrations and sleepless nights, the experiences of medical school will affirm that being a doctor is your life path. If you don't feel this way—if you spend most days in medical school feeling trapped and coerced—something is wrong. You need to give yourself the freedom to continue medical school or to walk away. Taking responsibility for this choice is hard, but it will help you to appreciate the experience of medical school more.

Certain things are out of your hands. During medical school, someone close to you may become ill. You may fail your first exam. The relationship you want desperately to work doesn't. This is a hard lesson (particularly for medical students) to learn: you cannot control everything by your choice. You cannot slow down time or cure every sickness. What you can do is choose how you react. This is the message of the Serenity Prayer: Accept what you cannot change, change what you can, and have the wisdom to know the difference.

2

EXCEL IN YOUR STUDIES

14. Repeat this Mantra:
P = M.D.

At the medical school I attended, we reminded ourselves of this saying frequently: P = M.D. In other words, as long as you pass ("P"), you'll become a doctor ("M.D.") This is not an acceptance of mediocrity, but an acknowledgement that our accomplishments are more than just academic.

If we are going to be truly good doctors, we need to start setting our own standards for our lives. That's why many schools are now on a pass/fail grading system. Beyond a certain amount of knowledge, the more you know does not correlate with being a better doctor. Some of the people who struggled to pass their exams in school are now the most insightful, compassionate, and competent doctors I know.

Good doctors are, first and foremost, good human beings. Your sanity and your peace of mind are just as important as your academics. Sometimes it will be difficult to remember this. In medical school, you'll see many people running frantic, worried, and forever falling short. Remind yourself that it doesn't have to be this way. And when all else fails, repeat your mantra: P = M.D.

15. CELEBRATE THE
SMALL VICTORIES

The tunnel of medical training is simply too long to wait for the light at the very end to celebrate. So celebrate the small victories—finishing your midterms, taking the Board exam, the end of a rotation. It's important to mark these accomplishments as you go along. Otherwise, medical school will become a string of overwhelming responsibilities and endless commitments.

One of the most insidious forms of stress in medical school is that you can never escape the feeling that you have something to do. You can't enjoy your free time because it's never really free. You are plagued with the guilty feeling that you have some school-related thing to do. In effect, you are never free.

That's why it's important to block some time off after each tiny accomplishment, and not allow yourself to do anything related to school. Forget the fact that you have another exam in one week, and many of your classmates are barely pausing to breathe before launching into the books again. You need to separate yourself from the demands of medical school for a period. These points of pause, of honoring your hard work and celebrating, are key to a sane and productive life.

16. GET ORGANIZED

You can learn to be organized. And in medical school, you have to. In the first year of medical school, you tackle hundreds of pages of information in a dozen different syllabi. Simply getting to the right clerkship at the right time can be a feat (don't laugh, it's harder than you think). In this setting, disorganization is incompatible with a sane life.

Develop a strategy for keeping yourself organized. For example, some students create elaborate filing systems or color code their notes. I used a master "to-do" list that I would tack on my fridge. I also bought a large agenda book and kept it on me at all times. Nowadays, people swear by their palm pilots.

Learn to forecast your needs. Take fifteen minutes each night to review your activities for the next day and prepare the materials that you need. Organize yourself before each new semester or rotation. These practices require some discipline at first. But it pays off in the end—in time saved and anxiety spared.

17. MISS SOME CLASSES

When I started medical school, a senior student advised me to *not* go to class. At the time I thought that this was flippant advice. Later, I realized there was a grain of truth in what he was saying. Eight hours a day in a classroom doesn't leave much time for other things in your life—not even for studying. Attending all your classes is a sure-fire way to be booked solid for the first two years.

Make some decisions about how to structure your education. Classes are valuable and necessary—to an extent. A lot of it depends on your style of learning and your school. Those schools with case-based learning curriculums have already drastically reduced lecture hours in place of small groups. Many traditional institutions, however, still have you sitting in a hard-backed wooden chair watching the next display of PowerPoint slides on the projector. It's no surprise that five minutes after the lights are dimmed, people start drifting off.

If you realize that lectures are just a time to catch up on your Z's, then don't waste your time. Attend those lectures that you think are particularly valuable. Most schools have lecture notes or syllabi that you can purchase with all the same information. For the highly motivated student who learns more efficiently on her own, missing some lectures could be the best choice for learning.

18. Study in Your Own Way

Each of us learns differently, and we need to study differently, too. For me, the library was torture. I'd rather be forced to sit and eat a plate full of cafeteria chicken livers than be stuck in that sterile building for more than a half hour. For someone else, the silence of the library is sheer bliss. In medical school, you will become an expert at studying. You'll see that the amount of time studying does not directly correlate with the amount of material learned. Sitting around drinking beers with friends while going over the layers of the artery is probably not going to be peak learning time.

Stick with your own groove when it comes to studying. If your mental clarity is highest in the early hours, rise with the sun. Don't stay up late force-feeding material when your intelligence wanes. Some of us can cram and still learn. For others, this is too nerve-racking. Study groups are always a good way to get a lot of different perspectives on the same material, and they are more enjoyable for a lot of people. But if your study group leaves you feeling panicked, you're probably doing more harm than benefit.

Paying attention to your own style of learning is the key to academic success in the first few years. With the right approach, studying will be as natural as eating—both productive and enjoyable.

19. If You Don't Pass an Exam, Move On

To incoming medical students, the prospect of failing an exam is terrifying. This is when you know you're green. The veteran medical students have long surpassed that fear. Taking exams is like a juggling act. When you keep adding more and more balls at increasing speeds, sooner or later one is going to drop. That's the day you fail your first exam.

I had one friend who failed her first anatomy exam. It was a climactic moment, when all of us were gathered around the list of scores outside the lab. I jumped in elation when I located the score next to my social security number, but then I found out that my friend had failed. She spent that night in tears, doubting herself, wondering whether she was really cut out for medical school. She persevered and proved to herself that she could do it. In the future, she faced other difficulties but it was never as hard as that first time. Failing an exam was an inconvenience and a disappointment, but it wasn't a devastating event. She had learned that one exam score couldn't make or break her.

My advice? Move on and lighten up. Failing an exam is not the end of the world. In the scheme of things, it's barely even a tremor. This should not be something you lose sleep over. You need to be able to take these things in stride. Remember my advice about developing staying power? Failing an exam is just another opportunity for you to strengthen your resolve. Believe it or not, it actually gets easier with time.

20. SETTLE DISPUTES EARLY

Problems will come from time to time. A personality clash with a resident. A dispute about an evaluation. A scheduling problem. Whatever it is, don't delay. The problem is usually not as big a deal if you catch it early and confront it in a forthright manner.

Most medical schools have an ombudsperson. This person's job is to mediate disputes between students and the administration. If your school doesn't have an ombudsperson, and you have a problem, seek the advice of a professor or a classmate that you trust. They can help you get a neutral perspective on the situation. More often than not, you can settle the issue with the appropriate person before it goes any further. As with any conflict mediation process, it's best to phrase things in terms of how you feel, rather than blaming or accusing others. The majority of disputes can be resolved simply by opening the channels of communication. If you reach a dead end, you may wish to seek help from people higher up.

If you make an effort to address problems at the onset, you will save yourself and others a lot of unnecessary emotional turmoil. Better to face a small problem now than a crisis later.

21. Write a Dread List

Many of us struggle with procrastination. We avoid the things that we dislike, until it becomes so uncomfortable or urgent that we have to face it. In medical school, this is a source of stress and anxiety that you can easily do away with. The answer is to write a dread list.

A dread list is everything that you are loathe to do—cracking the book to study for Boards, dealing with the pile of tickets on the floor of your car, or getting that funny bump examined at student health. These are the tasks that get pushed by the wayside in the hustle and bustle of life but eat away at your mind. These worries only grow when they are ignored.

Writing them down is the first step. From there, you can tick them off one by one. With every task completed or even started, you can feel your burden lighten. Keeping a regular dread list helps you to face your procrastination head on. So the next time you're feeling overwhelmed and unfocused, focus first on the things that you dread. It can only get better from there.

22. If in Doubt, Throw It Out

Is your must-read pile overflowing with articles from classes and clerkships? I'll let you in on a secret. If you don't read that article your resident gave you the same night, your chances of skimming even the abstract go down drastically. If you ignore it for a week, the opportunity is as good as gone (you've now accumulated a dozen other articles more pertinent to the current situation). If this is true for a clinically relevant review article, you can imagine your hunger to review your old notes on glomerular filtration rates after the fact.

The best strategy is this: Throw it out. If you keep all of your materials, you will quickly become overwhelmed and lose access to the most important things. Have confidence in what your brain has absorbed. Unless you consider a particular article or syllabus the quintessential reference on the subject, get rid of it. You can always look up the material later. People tend to be most nostalgic about research articles, amassing a huge filing system for when they are interns and residents (and can torture their own third-year student). If you do this, go through your files regularly. This will refresh your memory about what you have and allow you to clean out the obscure, the irrelevant, and the outdated.

23. Ask for Academic Help

A common theme throughout this book is to never give up. There are always options, usually more than you can imagine. A true survivor seeks them out, particularly when it comes to your studies.

Don't be bashful about asking for academic help. Schools anticipate that people may need extra help and make provisions for this. The best resource is your professor. Make an appointment and let her know you need help. Many professors hold special review groups for students having difficulty. At least the professor can connect you with others who will help. People will come to your rescue, as long as you are actively seeking help.

Your biggest enemy is pride. I've seen this silent beast take down more than a few people. Pride keeps us from speaking up or seeking the help we need—until it's too late. Have the strength to recognize your difficulties early. There's no shame in recognizing your weaknesses. All of us struggle in some area. The real question is how you're going to face that challenge. If you believe in yourself, you'll know that you're worth all the assistance that others can offer.

24. APPRECIATE YOUR TEACHERS

Many people will teach you in medical school—basic science professors, interns, and attending doctors. These people have worked hard in their fields, and as a result, they know a lot. Their willingness to share with you is a great gift. This gift should be honored by each of us. What better way to honor our knowledge than to show our appreciation to our teachers!

Appreciating your teachers keeps you humble—a goal we should strive for both in our studies and in life. At times, however, we medical students can be egoistic. I remember being in a small group with a doctor who was volunteering his time to teach. He was a kind man, but his teaching style was less than inspiring. After the class, everyone moaned how he had wasted their time. They walked down the hall laughing, complaining, and insulting—all at his expense. This type of criticism was not unusual. Medical school, with all the demands placed upon us, can make us demanding as well. Imagine, however, if we were to react this way every time that we received a gift that we didn't like. It seems ridiculous to get angry and insulting with your friend because the sweater she gave you is itchy and too small. Why, then, do we allow ourselves to be so harsh and unappreciative of the gift of teaching?

As students, we need to restore the balance toward appreciation of our education and our teachers. If you have a complaint about a teacher or a certain class, funnel it into your school's curriculum committee. Complaining as you walk down the hall does nothing but spread ingratitude. On the other hand, if you enjoy a particular lecture, drop the professor a note to let them know how much you learned. Nominate your favorite teachers for awards, and support them when they make advances in their fields. A little appreciation goes a long way for those who do much work for our benefit.

3

PARTICIPATE IN YOUR COMMUNITY

25. Nurture Your Friendships

Let this rule be a warning to every new medical student. You need your friends. They will sustain you when times are tough and remind you that there's more to life than medical school. Besides, other than your class-mates, you probably won't make too many new friends during this time. A booming social life is just not one of the highlights of medical school. That's why it's important to nurture the friendships that you have.

Medical students are prone to what I call "sudden neglect syndrome." We open up the doors to medical school, and like a tornado it consumes our lives. We use the busyness of medical school as an excuse to neglect other meaningful areas of our lives. The aftermath of this storm isn't pretty. It takes only a short time to lose touch with friends and to become isolated. Four years down the road, you realize that you don't have too many people in your life. That's a lonely road, and I've seen many people walk down it (many of them scrambling in their fourth year to get married . . .).

Sometimes, even the smallest efforts make a difference. Try writing a short note to an old friend. It takes less than ten minutes, and it means much more than you know. A community of friends, whether it be within five miles of you, or scattered around the globe, is a crucial part of our well-being. Medical school can never replace it.

26. FIND A ROLE MODEL

Having role models in medical school makes a tremendous difference in your life. These are the doctors who you aspire to become and the ones you rely on in times of need. They are the people who believe in you, even more than you believe in yourself. Most important, they remind you of everything good about medicine.

We've all heard the stats on how few doctors, if they could do it all over again, would choose medicine as a career. It's discouraging. That's why we need role models in medicine—to defy the trends we most fear. Your role model is the person who loves being a doctor. She is the surgeon that proves you can have a life outside of the operating room. Or the family doctor that still does house calls. These people help to restore our perspective and renew our idealism about medicine.

They are also doctors who understand your experience. When you reach an impasse, they can provide the insight that you need to go on. This is different than the support you receive from family and friends. It is the understanding of someone who has been there and has made it through. Sometimes, this is just what we need.

27. MAKE FRIENDS IN YOUR CLASS

Making friends in medical school is one of the ways that these four years can actually be enjoyable. If you have a couple of good friends in your class, you can make it through anything. When I started medical school in San Francisco, I didn't have a place to live. At the orientation, one of my classmates, a demure Vietnamese woman, tapped me on the shoulder saying, "I overheard you need somewhere to stay. You can stay with me." I was perplexed by her offer; she didn't seem to be the type of person that I would usually attract or befriend. Huong was graceful and quiet, with a traditional look about her. I was the opposite—offbeat and outspoken. That night, I brought my boxes over to her house, and we've been best friends ever since.

Friendships in medical school are similar to those you hear about in the military, forged in the barracks of war. I don't mean to sound dramatic, but it's true. The experience you share in medical school is strenuous, unusual, and intense. Many other people, even spouses and family, won't be able to relate to what you're going through during this time. The people who do understand are your classmates.

This understanding carries you a long way. I don't know how I would have survived medical school without my friend Huong. When I had a bad day, she would remind me that there was more to life than medical school. She taught me the true meaning of perseverance. She echoed back my own hopes and fears about being a doctor. She forced me out of slumber at 3 A.M. to make sure I looked at the pregnancy hormone cycle one last time. Whether I had problems with schoolwork or with life, she was there.

Take advantage of the time in medical school to make friends in your class. Appreciate their quirks and enjoy their company. Get to know each others' friends and spouses. Support one another. These may be some of the best and strongest friendships of your life.

28. Do Service

In medical school, it is tempting to hole yourself up with your books and your classmates and seclude yourself from all life outside. After one year, you already begin to feel the separation—you are less interested in world events (no time to read the paper), all conversations are geared to medicine, and you look at the people who have time to sit leisurely in cafés as an odd indulgent breed. The path of least resistance leads to this scenario. If you don't want this to be your life, you need to poke some holes in the medical school bubble.

One way to maintain connection with the outside world is through service. It reminds you of a bigger picture—of children learning to read, of rivers flowing, of a man dying. It opens up your world and flushes it out with stories, different values, and a new perspective. And it connects you with the power of your own life. It shows you that every little thing you do, every choice, makes a difference in this world.

Time and time again, throughout medical school, this rule saved me. Every Tuesday night, a number of us medical students would teach boys at juvenile hall. Usually, we would give lessons on what we were studying—the immune system, sexually transmitted diseases, muscles. We would bring in preserved brains and skeletons to show them. Afterward, we would talk about life—about their hopes for the future, a court case, their friend who was just shot and killed. These young people shared much with us. They appreciated our attention and our belief in them. When I was blasted with exams, and everyone was up all night cramming in more information, I would go to the detention center. Often, I wanted to skip it so I could study. But I knew that someone else depended on me. My world was larger than medical school. The next day, I would walk into the exam, knowing a lot less about collagen vascular diseases but a lot more about life. This approach never failed me; much to my surprise, I'd always pass. I swear to this day, it must have been the angels of service looking over me.

29. PRIORITIZE FAMILY

The loss of personal relationships during medical school is not inevitable. In fact, it is a choice. If you value your family, you need to make them a priority.

Having witnessed many different medical school relationships, including my own, I can attest to the "get what you give" theory. Several of my married classmates were frustrated over not seeing their spouses for days on end, yet I would see them waste hours at the hospital engaged in small talk. No relationship, whether intimate, parent-child, or sibling, can withstand complete neglect. The people who are able to sustain healthy relationships are those that prioritize this aspect of their lives. Not surprisingly, these are the students who tend to be the most content and less scathed by the medical school experience.

To care for our own well-being, we need to anchor ourselves to the ones we love the most. Our families know us the best, and if we take the time to include them, they can be far more helpful than the graveyard-shift nurse we too often confide in.

For those of you who have children during your training, I pass along this comment from a classmate. Referring to her one-year-old baby, she said, "She screams and dances with joy when I come home, and erases in one moment all the pains of the day."

30. EXPERIENCE YOUR TOWN

Sometimes, it can be tough to wrench ourselves away from the campus. After all, as medical students, our whole world revolves around that space—the lecture halls, the hospital, the library. After the first year, you've eaten in the cafeteria so much, you think that drained peas and frozen yogurt are the best of modern cuisine. This is when you know that you're suffering from environmental myopia. You need to get out.

There are many creative ways to see the town that are easy, fun, and time-conscious. When I first started medical school, my classmate and I decided we would explore a different bar or nightclub each week (a classic sign of first-semester medical student denial and escapism). It didn't last more than six months, but in that time we saw a lot of San Francisco (and landed ourselves in some strange dives). For the more traditional medical student, the weekly Latino transvestite beauty show may not top the list of activities to explore. Maybe a monthly Sunday afternoon cultural outing would be more your style.

You can double up studying with exploration of the city. One of my classmates would bring his books and read in different cafés around the city. He may have had his head buried in a Netter diagram, but at least he could experience the flow of life outside of medical school (it's amazing how gross anatomy turns heads). It may not seem like efficient studying, but if he is more inspired in these spaces, he will also be more motivated. This doesn't work for everyone, but if you like to make studying fun, this may be something to try.

31. Don't Date Classmates

In my first month of medical school, some of the women doctors on the faculty held a dinner for incoming medical students. One by one, they stood up to introduce themselves to us. The first one began by telling a story how she married her anatomy lab partner. A few introductions passed, and another woman stood up and said she also married the man who was her anatomy lab partner. One other woman rose, gave her spiel about her specialty and practice. As an afterthought, she added, "You may not believe this, but I also married my anatomy lab partner." I laughed with the rest, but inside I was feeling queasy. Finally, the last woman spoke. She said, "Unlike everyone else, I married a carpenter. That way, at the end of a hard day, we have something real to talk about."

The world of medicine has a way of boiling our identity down to one thing: being a medical student (or a resident, or a doctor). Not dating your classmates is just one way of making sure that your world doesn't close in on you. Ultimately, if you do happen to find the person of your dreams, and coincidentally, by extraordinary chance, that person happens to be looking across the cadaver from you, then so be it. At the very least, cultivate other pastimes that you do together—bike riding, cooking, or poetry. Come up with creative ways to share other parts of yourselves and your lives.

There are other reasons not to date classmates—like the fact that you have to see these people constantly for the next four years. Romance is messy. We all know what a tumultuous breakup feels like. The last thing you want is to be partnered with your ex for a surgery rotation, or watch him get cuddly with another classmate. What's more—people gossip. And talk about distractions . . .

Dating outside of school keeps your academic world out of your personal life. It also gives you a reason to do all the other things that keep your life fresh and fulfilling—exploring your city, traveling, or going out dancing. Keep your eyes open and who knows who you'll find!

32. Share Your Talents

In medical school, a friend of mine organized a show for our classmates, entitled "Something About Us." The purpose was to share whatever it was that was unique about us. When she asked me what I would do, I scanned my brain and thought of the traditional talents, like playing the flute or painting. I told her I didn't really have a talent. She looked at me dumbfounded. "Don't you dance?" "Yeah," I retorted jokingly, "in clubs. That doesn't count." She returned with a stare that made me know immediately I was going to be up there making some kind of ridiculous fool of myself.

I wound up doing an "interpretive" dance performance to the music of Talk-Talk. Not your garden-variety talent act, but neither was anyone else's. Sure, one guy was a classical pianist (playing since five years old) and another held the final note of Magdelena for about three breath-taking minutes, but there were also people who showed slides from their travels, or made Indian food, or simply read their favorite short story. It didn't matter what you did, or how "skilled" you were at something, it was the fact that you shared. The result was a picture of this eclectic group of people who all came together to study medicine, each as unique and special as distinct coins from around the world.

Before this performance, like most people, I had a narrow definition of the word "talent." I thought to myself, "I can't dance." The ironic thing is, ever since this experience, I consider myself a dancer. I dance any chance that I get—in dance class, in festivals, in clubs. It's something I do, and I love it. To share this with others is one of the great joys of my life.

In medical school, we need to challenge ourselves to share more than just medical facts. Your talent could be in the arts, or maybe it's a special ability to visualize all the arteries in the body. Whatever it is, share it with others—your classmates, your patients, your professors. You will find that this simple act of sharing has the ability to inspire and touch lives, including your own.

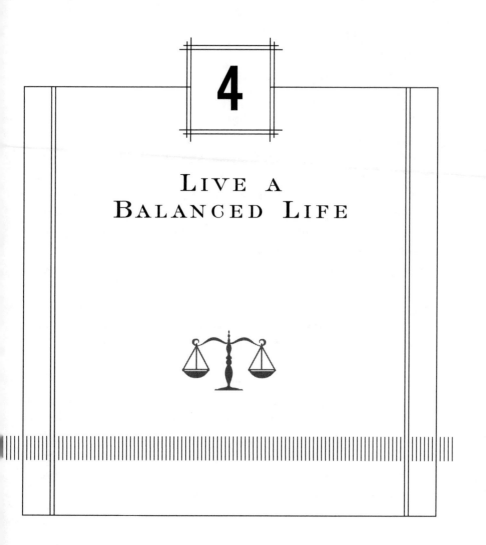

4

LIVE A
BALANCED LIFE

33. Pick Up a New Hobby

The healthiest, happiest medical students seem to be those that realize they are not just a student of medicine, but a student of life. Dating, traveling, and adopting new hobbies are all what I call "signs of life" in the medical student world. It stands to reason that those who are actively broadening their life experience would experience less damage from the sometimes harsh medical training.

One of my favorite peers in my class was particularly adventurous. In only four years, I saw her take up salsa dancing, singing, playing the violin, and gymnastics. The gymnastics really impressed me since I had long lost my own limberness. She raved about how it felt to do gymnastics after so many years and how her goal was to do a back-handspring by the time she turned thirty. I often laugh when I think of her standing in a line of six year olds, all with matching leotards.

A new hobby can do wonders for your state of mind and enjoyment of life. If you are like most medical students, you designed your path to medicine with a great deal of focus. In the past, you had little time for frivolous pursuits. Now is the time to give yourself some leeway. Ironically, if you allow yourself the freedom of a child, you'll actually be a more grounded adult—and a better doctor!

34. EXERCISE

This rule makes it onto my top-ten list. I am convinced that if you exercise regularly, no matter who you are, your life will be better. Breaking a sweat elevates your mood, and makes you feel healthy and strong. It reduces stress and gives your mind a break. I even find that when I exercise I eat better.

This is not a secret for most medical students. At the end of the day, after sitting in a hard-backed wooden chair for eight hours, most students break for the gym. You can almost see the mental tension just oozing from the pores. Most medical centers have fitness facilities that are free and convenient. If your school doesn't, then find an alternative that's easy for you.

Exercising regularly is a discipline. It's best to establish regular times and stick to it, no matter what. It may help to join a class or exercise with a friend. Many of us tell ourselves that we're too busy. I do the opposite. I tell myself I'm too busy not to exercise. After all, I know that an hour of exercise will increase my productivity and efficiency throughout the day.

35. LIVE WITHIN YOUR MEANS

One of the smartest things you can do in medical school is to live within your means. This is another way of saying "live simply." In the next four years, you will have a lot of things on your plate. Be careful about the extra responsibilities and concerns that you take on.

Every decision we make either complicates our life or simplifies it. One common way of complicating your life is to overspend—charging to the limit on credit cards, taking out more loans, moving into apartments you can't afford. In the moment, you may believe that having more things will give you happiness. In reality, I have watched many people become miserable as a result of their own consumerism.

Every new thing you accumulate is a commitment—cell phones, pagers, water purifiers, skiing equipment, even medical books. Each time, you need to ask yourself if you are willing to put in the investment of time and energy required to sustain your belongings. I think of this every time I am lugging huge sacks of clothes to my car to bring to the laundromat. At first, I curse the fact that I have such a ridiculous amount of clothes, and then I think to myself, "If only I had a washer and dryer . . ." It's funny how our minds work. The more we have, the more we think we need. We buy stuff to take care of our stuff, all the while thinking that the next item will make our lives easier or better. In fact, the opposite is true!

The key to living a happy life is to live a simple life. In medical school, the most precious commodity is your time and your peace of mind. Be cautious about how you exchange these commodities for others. What good is having a fancy car in medical school if you're going to have to moonlight every free moment in residency to pay for it? Why buy a ton of medical texts if you have trouble finding what you need when you need it?

One day, you may choose to have all these things. For now, enjoy the freedom of being a low-budget student. Take out a minimal amount of loans. Live close to school, and ride your bike or walk, rather than drive. Ask yourself what you truly need to be happy, and invest in those few things. I think that you'll find that in having less, you actually have *more* of what really matters.

36. Keep a Secret Spot

A "secret spot" is a special place outside that you revisit time and time again—a place where you can collect your bearings or find inspiration. My spot is under a large eucalyptus tree overlooking the housing projects and the highway. To others, it may not be the most scenic, but for me with the grass blowing and the sweet fragrance of eucalyptus in the air, it's a sanctuary. Yours may be by a small creek or in a park.

Some medical students are able to manage crazy schedules and demands with some semblance of inner peace. It's not because they are wired that way; they take conscious actions to create inner peace. Keeping a secret spot is one way to begin this process, to make a commitment to yourself and your spirit.

Go to your secret spot every day, even if it's only for fifteen minutes. Don't bring anything else to do. Focus on the things around you. Be aware of the plants growing in the area and the different birds that you hear. Pay attention to how your spot changes with the seasons. The longer that you sit in that place the more you will notice and become a part of the environment. After a while, you will come to know that place of earth well, and your connection will grow.

This connection will bring you peace of mind that resonates throughout the day. In the rest of your life, there may be tremendous responsibilities or worries. But when you are at your secret spot, you can leave those things behind. This is the time that you dedicate to yourself. The benefits are immense.

37. Treat Yourself

Survival in medical school is really a matter of appreciating small joys. A good night's sleep. A new CD every once in a while. A good basketball game. For all the work that you are putting in, you deserve it.

The only one who is responsible for treating you well is yourself. If you're lucky, you have a spouse or partner that will help with this. Otherwise, you have to be your own best friend. Even if you are on a student budget, don't be frugal with the things that you really enjoy. If a weekend skiing will help you collect your bearings, go for it! The cost of these things are small in comparison to what they give you (unless of course, your treat is a new Lexus).

Doing things for yourself is really a question of self-maintenance. You need to maintain all aspects of your life—your studies, your financial matters, and your happiness. Make a contribution to your happiness on a regular basis. Treat yourself.

38. Don't Have Affairs
(with Anyone!)

This advice makes the top-ten list for those of you who are married or have serious partners. Think twice before you have an affair. I've watched a few people make this mistake, and it wreaks havoc on lives.

We all know that medical training takes a toll on our relationships. Time devoted to medical training competes with relationship time. In the next four years, you'll spend most of your time with classmates. Understandably, at times, you may feel closer to them than your partner. You share a similar routine, the same language, a common struggle. Add to this the mental stress of medical school and a little discontentment with your current relationship, and it's not too hard to fall into another person's arms.

These affairs never quite fulfill what we may be seeking. Ultimately, they lead to further deceit, more relationship distress, and greater isolation. This turmoil compromises our ability to function in all aspects of our life, including academically.

As a rule of thumb, don't evaluate relationships when your life is in duress (i.e., no heavy discussions post-call). When you act out of emotional lability or confusion, you don't do what is best for yourself or others. Wait until you have some clarity of mind and more time to make decisions about relationships. This approach will keep you honest and protect you from rash decisions with potentially devastating consequences.

39. Get Up Early

The way you start your day largely determines the course of it. All of us have had the experience of oversleeping and bolting out the door ten minutes before a lecture starts. You feel hurried, you forget your stethoscope, and you go through the day feeling chaotic. Rising early and creating a ritual to start the day is one way to build more sanity and calmness into your life.

I recommend a three-pronged morning ritual for medical students. Begin with thankfulness. This could be a few minutes that you spend watching the sky lighten. Or a prayer of gratitude (thank you, God, for awakening me to one more day of great torment, I mean blessing). Second, take time for something you enjoy—having a leisurely cup of tea, going for a morning jog, or writing. Finally, spend a few moments preparing for the day—writing down a to-do list or gathering your materials.

It may be difficult at first to rise early, but I guarantee you the results will be astonishing. No matter what difficulties face you in the day, you'll be able to approach them with greater assurance and equanimity.

40. Practice What You Fear Most

How often do you avoid doing something that you dread, only to make the situation worse? How often do you say "I can't do that" and refuse to try? Fear stops us from doing a lot of things in life, and in medical school that can be a real problem.

A friend of mine had a great analogy for fear. He said fear was like demons made of cardboard. From far away, they are frightful and imposing, casting dark shadows on our lives. But once you approach them, you realize they aren't real at all. With a touch of the finger, they fall over. I think of this often. It reminds me that if I really want to overcome my fear, I can't run away. I need to advance in its direction, and see it for what it truly is—an imposter.

To practice what you fear most is the quickest way to resolve your fears. In medical school, I hated confrontations with people. If I had a problem with a nurse, I would avoid him, only making the situation more uncomfortable. One day I realized the source of my avoidance: the fear of not being liked. From then on, before confronting someone I'd tell myself, "It's okay if this person doesn't like me." I'd go over all the reasons why confronting this person was the right thing to do. When I actually faced the person I was avoiding, I felt a sense of liberation. Each time I did this, it got easier.

If you are able to tackle your fears on a day-to-day basis, you will grow immensely. Underneath each of your fears is a hidden potential of the person you can be. Make today the day to face what you fear most.

41. SLEEP

Getting regular sleep is absolutely essential to your health, your happiness, and your success as a medical student. Unfortunately, I didn't learn this principle until much later on in my medical training. I used to regularly deprive myself of sleep, excited that I could get more hours out of the day. For me, this meant more hours to be productive, to have fun, to deal with crisis. I was so proud of my sleep deprivation that I would insist to my friends that it is one of the miracles of the body—to simply adjust to what you give it.

Years later, I can evaluate this claim in a broader perspective. I know that the studying that I did in the wee hours of the morning was often my least efficient. I lost hours of lecture time dozing off, leaving me with indecipherable chicken scratch for notes. I was often out of sorts, not eating, and forgetting things. I also got sick more often in medical school than any other time in my life. I may have gained more time awake, but I know I didn't make the best use of that time.

Sleeping will drastically improve the quality of your life. Now that I sleep 8 hours a night, I realize that I am a more pleasant, well-adjusted person. I don't feel like I am racing against a clock to fit more things in than the day can hold. I'm more realistic with the time that I have. And I don't need to rely on substances like caffeine to keep me going (see #92).

Most medical students believe that chronic sleep deprivation is simply part of the picture. At some points, this is true, like when you're on the labor ward and your patients are in labor all night. In the first two years, however, you shouldn't be robbing yourself of sleep. You can plan ahead. Find the study routines that are most effective and stick to them. If you're falling asleep in lecture, give it up, go home, and nap.

When everything around you is in high demand, sleep is an oasis. It is also the cornerstone of a balanced and peaceful life. If you are sleeping well, trying to understand the gazillion pathways of immune complements will be that much easier.

42. CARPE DIEM! (SEIZE THE DAY!)

From a young age, I was schooled in the principle of delayed gratification. According to my parents, this was the key to success. Simply postpone your pleasure now, and you'll be rewarded later on. Much of my life had been based on this precept, right up to the first day of medical school.

I now offer the opposite advice: *Carpe diem* (seize the day)! Three decades of living have provided me with sufficient evidence to debunk the delayed gratification theory. How many of the things that you planned for yesterday are actually true today? Life is uncertain; people change; tragedies happen. I once read that Tibetan monks, when they go to sleep at night, extinguish even the coals of the fire, because they don't know if that sleep is their last. Most of us, particularly in medical school, live quite the opposite; we plan our lives through the next decade. We forget what it's like to be in the present. In fact, I think many of us are scared of the present, scared to look at ourselves and ask what it would take to make us happy right now. We've been told if we live too much for today, we'll regret it tomorrow. I've never actually seen this happen, never watched someone be miserable by living too much in the moment. On the other hand, I've witnessed a lot of misery because of postponing dreams, planning too much and too long for an uncertain tomorrow.

What this boils down to, in a practical sense, is that you can and should live during medical school. Uproot that outdated notion of sacrifice. There's no magical reward on the other side. Do everything and anything to find happiness in the moment. Take advantage of opportunities that arise—whether it's the martial arts classes that you always wanted to take, or the opportunity to work in Africa for the summer. Push yourself to take risks, to try new things, to see new sights. Ask yourself what it takes to bring you peace, and do it. It is possible to achieve this, even with the limited time constraints of medical school. You just need to put your mind to it.

43. Take a Break

Sometimes when we're in the midst of something we lose perspective. This is true whether it's a relationship, a research project, or a chapter in your physiology book. Taking a break from the situation is often the most productive thing you can do.

I learned this lesson from one of my anatomy professors. I had been furiously dissecting the right arm of a cadaver, looking for the subclavian vein. I was determined to find it, cutting and pulling, when my professor ordered me to step down. "Give it a break," she said. "You've lost your perspective." She scolded me that by being too close, I had lost the larger picture.

These words are true for many situations. When you get yourself worked up over a particular concept that you don't understand, or you feel like you're drowning in all the responsibilities of a certain rotation, simply take a break. It doesn't have to be a trip to the Bahamas. Sometimes a walk in the park is sufficient (see #36). Perhaps it is a weekend that you set aside to not do any school work. Often, we convince ourselves that we can't take a break, that we'd fall behind in our school work, or something horrible would happen. Usually, it's just the opposite: We achieve more with a strategic break because we return to the task renewed and with a fresh perspective.

5

LEARN TO HEAL

44. Remain Open

In medicine, you encounter many difficult and painful circumstances. How do you reconcile sending a pregnant woman back to the streets to live? How do you face the agony of the parents whose thirteen-year-old child was shot and killed? The natural response is to build walls to protect yourself from pain. In the end, however, if you close yourself off, you won't feel the emotions that renew you—joy, intimacy, and laughter.

In order to find meaning in our work, we need to be open and available emotionally. Remaining open is not easy; it requires a disciplined effort—sitting through the pain, asking difficult questions of patients, or taking time to show that you care. It is an emotional choice that we make each day, both for our patients and for ourselves.

A friend of mine who is now a pediatric resident recently told me about an experience he had on pediatric oncology, a particularly dreaded rotation by residents. Darryl had been taking care of a teenage boy, Johnny, who was dying of cancer and having multiple awful reactions to the drug treatments. The boy was so depressed that he refused to leave his bed for many weeks. One night, at 3 A.M. Darryl found himself in Johnny's room playing battleships. They had agreed upon a wager: if Darryl lost, he had to sing a song of Johnny's choice while dancing in front of all the pediatric nurses. Darryl recounted the humiliating and inspiring experience of paging all the floor nurses to Johnny's room as he swayed and sang to "Come on baby, light my fire . . ." The next day, Johnny was so happy that he was moving about the floor with his IV, and when they gave him his daily dose of amphotericin (an antibiotic), for the first time ever, he didn't have a violent reaction of rigors.

Sometimes, the things that we expect to be awful turn out to have many pleasant surprises. Even the things that seem terrible and unfair offer a host of lessons. If we are able to stop resisting and embrace the moment, then we will be able to find the lesson in the experience. A few weeks after the song and dance, Johnny died. When Darryl was told, he sat down, in front of the whole medical team, and cried. He had allowed himself to be close and to care. He had passed through the rotation he feared, taken the responsibility he had previously resisted, and felt all the lessons. He said to me, "Right then I felt like I was truly living."

45. Accept that You Are Not in Control

Several times I have been in the presence of a pregnant woman who was smoking. This is disturbing given everything I know about how bad it is for her as well as for her fetus. Sometimes I feel protective of the fetus and judgmental of the mother. Other times I feel compassion for the woman and am able to trust that things will be okay, or simply let go if they are not. What is the role of the medical student in this scenario? What if she were using more serious drugs? How involved should you become?

As a medical student and a caretaker, you need to do what you can and let go of the rest. Many times, you will witness people who are tearing themselves up. You will be confronted with situations that are sad and downright frustrating. If you believe that you are personally responsible for saving the world, you will quickly feel defeated.

Neither should you feel helpless. The things you can do are quite powerful. For example, a patient may develop an abscess from IV heroin use. In one visit, you can open the man's abscess and provide antibiotics to help it heal. You can educate him about dirty needles and heroin use, and even refer him to detox programs (see #47). And you can believe that, if he really desires, he is capable of changing his life around. As long as you do what you can and continue to have faith in your patients, you will have an impact.

Accepting that you are not in control is hard for many of you who are used to finding solutions and fixing things. It is true that the man may shoot heroin the same day he leaves the hospital. You can't do anything to stop it. Sometimes, however, the greatest thing you can do is accept your own limitations. That way, you have no reason to be angry at your patients or yourself. You simply do the best you can—and allow others the freedom to live their lives.

46. Pay Attention to the Spirit

Many people who face death or life-threatening illness discover a deeper view of life and the hereafter. As a medical student, you have a front row seat in this discovery. If you pay attention to the spirit, the experience will transform and deepen your life as well.

Several studies demonstrate the power of faith in healing. To some, this suggests the power of belief. To others it is the power of the divine. Whatever the etiology, faith has an impact on a patient's well-being. It is an important part of people's lives, and it plays a critical role in their illness. This faith represents an untapped potential for renewal and healing of our patients.

As a doctor-in-training, you are in a position to open the dialogue about spirituality. Few patients are bold enough to talk about this otherwise. They may be afraid to share their views with you or to open themselves to misunderstanding. If you show that you are willing to listen, you'll be amazed how much they will confide.

It's not important that you share the same belief system as your patient. One of my classmates who is Buddhist told me a story about a Christian patient who was dying of colon cancer. When she first met him, he was angry and resistant, often yelling at her as well as the nurses. In her visits, she asked him questions about his life and beliefs

about death. She shared prayers in her faith and encouraged
practice his own. Before he died, he told her, "You are somebody l
that I had become." Shortly after, his demeanor changed: He was qu ʒʋ
and loving with his wife and friends. He had found some peace in the
midst of dying.

47. Be an Educator

As physicians, we must educate our patients. All the medical facts and knowledge are only valuable if it helps people to live healthier lives. To learn to teach effectively, therefore, is a core objective of the medical school years.

Teaching your patients is not simply downloading information. As a physician, you have to find a way to create interest around the topic that you are teaching and deliver it at the right moment. A young man who is drinking excessively may not care about the fact that alcoholism will lead to liver disease in a decade. So trash the lecture on liver cirrhosis. He may be more interested in knowing that alcoholism leads to impotence. That's when you go into the details of how it happens—the hormonal changes, the inability to maintain an erection, the lack of drive. The ultimate message is that he needs to quit drinking alcohol.

Our patients have incredible trust in us as physicians and give credence to what we say. We should be honored by this role and use it wisely. Although you cannot control what your patients do once they leave your presence, you can arm them with information that enables them to make informed decisions about their lives. The few moments that you spend educating your patients may make all the difference ten years down the road.

48. NEVER TAKE AWAY HOPE

One of the greatest medicines that we can give our patients is hope. So many times, we are confronted by circumstances that seem hopeless. A person may be ravaged by cancer in the most advanced stage. Still, we should never take away hope.

As a medical student, you will often be the one who is explaining the prognosis to the patient. On more than one occasion, a patient has turned to me and asked point-blank, "Am I going to die?" If all evidence points in that direction, what do you say?

To maintain hope does not mean to deceive the patient. We can be honest, while admitting that we don't know. As many times as doctors have seen people succumb to fatal disease, we have also witnessed at least one miracle. I'll never forget the day that I saw one of our patients, a ninety-three-year-old man who had suffered at least six bouts of pneumonia on a respirator in the ICU for six months, recover inexplicably and walk out of the hospital. These experiences remind us, that no matter what the odds, there is reason to have hope.

As a medical student, you can help patients to find hope where all seems lost. If their religious beliefs provide solace, support this—even if these beliefs are different from your own (see #46). Hope doesn't always have to be focused on recovery; perhaps you can help them accept their new situation. A young girl who has just had her leg amputated may find hope in talking with another young person who is living well under similar circumstances. Hope is a powerful medicine— whether to heal or to endure the pain. I am reminded of the last line in the *Shawshank Redemption* by Stephen King: "Remember that hope is a good thing, maybe the best of things, and no good thing ever dies."

49. DRINK SOME BARIUM

How can we have compassion for our patients if we don't know what they're going through? It's easy enough to hand someone a pint of liquid charcoal, but to actually consume that stuff is another feat altogether. The least that we can do, as budding doctors, is to make efforts to experience "the other side."

I can't say I've ever lost a spouse to cancer, or struggled with crack addiction, or been a single mother who is homeless. I hope that I don't ever have to go through those experiences. However, there are other, more mundane aspects of hospital care that it may benefit us to experience. In one medical school, it's actually part of the curriculum to have medical students sleep in the hospital and experience a routine day. I imagine the students being woken abruptly at 5 A.M. for a blood draw, reawakened at 6 A.M. for rounds, peered over by a crew of six people with cold stethoscopes, then delivered a breakfast of half-warm eggs with ham slices.

Most of you won't have the benefit of such a curriculum. I encourage you, however, to create those experiences for yourself. Think of it as an experiment and an adventure. Do you have the opportunity to go through a CT scan? By all means, see how terrifying that tube can be. Wonder why it's so difficult for people to get the barium down? Try a sample! Curious if those little shocks on the EMG hurt? Attach a few electrodes to your arm!

This may seem radical, but it's minor in comparison to what patients experience. You'll never really understand what the person is going through, but at least you are aware of some of the suffering. If anything, these small experiments will give you greater appreciation of your own life and the fortune of having good health. And this understanding can help you to relate to your patients in a more compassionate way.

50. USE COMMON LANGUAGE WITH YOUR PATIENTS

In medical school, we learn thousands of new words—words like idiopathic, epistaxis, hepatomegaly. We learn even more abbreviations—CHF, EOMI, MRI. It's no wonder when we talk it sounds like we're in another country. Medical professionals understand one another, but the rest of the world is clueless. That's why it's important, as medical students, to see ourselves as translators for patients.

Each of us needs to make a conscious effort to speak to our patients in common language. Try to remember how difficult it was for you the first time on the wards. Remember how nerve-racking it was to decipher the code language in medical records. You can imagine how a patient feels when the attending physician states that the bilateral pitting edema has increased to 3+. It's a whole lot easier if we just say "your ankles are more swollen."

Medical language isn't just different; it's scary. If you're a patient, you hold on to every word that the doctors say. Saying something is "erythematous" can be shocking; the word "red" is a lot kinder. Our patients often feel alienated when they are in the doctor's office or at the hospital. We should be conscious not to aggravate these feelings by using a foreign language as well.

Using common language with patients is an act of awareness. As medical students, we need to remember where we come from and not get lost in esoteric medical culture. This is a gift we give to ourselves *and* to our patients.

51. DEVELOP INNER CALM

We all know what it's like to be around frantic, socially inept doctors. It's not a pleasant experience, *especially* if you are the patient. In order to spare your patients any more discomfort than they are already experiencing, you should cultivate inner calm. This calm is what will separate the truly fine doctors (and medical students) from the rest. The importance of developing inner calm in practicing medicine is best illustrated by a story of two very different experiences I had in the delivery room during my Ob/Gyn rotation.

There was a Mexican woman who had been through eighteen hours of hard labor. The pregnancy was high risk, so there was a crowd of doctors around, including pediatric residents, watching me deliver the baby. It was all going smoothly until the actual moment when the baby squeezed out and was in my arms. I turned to reach for an instrument, and suddenly the cord avulsed (broke). Blood started spurting everywhere. From the head of the bed I could hear the shrill voice of the second-year resident, filled with panic and fury, *"Claaamppppp! Claaaaamppp!"* I froze. Again, and again, she shrieked, *"Clamp,"* and each time I became more debilitated. I stood there paralyzed amidst streams of blood and spinning faces until someone grabbed the infant from my arms and took over. The baby turned out to be okay, but I still couldn't shake the horror of the experience. That night, I crawled into bed still wearing my bloody socks, pulled the covers over my head, and cried.

It took me a while before I could get up the nerve to attempt another delivery. It was nearing the end of my rotation, and I wanted to get another chance. The second delivery was a sure-fire one—the third child, healthy mother, uncomplicated labor. The delivery went off like a breeze. The baby came out, was clamped, and suctioned. The placenta came out easily. Then came the blood. The attending doctor turned to me in a soft voice, "Okay, you're doing good. Now, massage the belly." More gushes of blood came. I started to panic, and again her voice soothed me: "Okay, doing good . . . that's a lot of blood . . . breathe . . . Okay, now she's hemorrhaging . . . let's give her 8 of Pitocin . . . keep massaging . . ." And on she went, as buckets of blood poured all over us, giving gentle orders, soothing the patient, and quelling my anxiety so I could continue to care for the patient. A half-hour later, the bleeding was controlled, and even though we were in dire straits for a while, all of us remained calm and collected. For the patient, it turned out to be a peaceful delivery.

In each of these situations, there was a crisis, as often happens in medicine. Our ability to handle that crisis, to interact with colleagues, and to deal with the patient all depends on our ability to stay calm. Strive to be like this latter doctor who, by keeping her composure, was able to inspire confidence in everyone around her.

52. Spend Time with Your Sickest Patients

If you really want to learn to be a healer, you need to spend time with the sickest patients. Ironically, these are the patients that we, as doctors, often avoid. They are the ones for whom all our medical treatments have failed, or who continue to decline despite our best efforts. It is these very sick patients, the ones beyond hope, that we tend to pass quickly on rounds. It is these people that, once they die, we move away from without even acknowledging to one another their existence.

Most of us are afraid of people who are dying. Yet, these people are often the greatest teachers of life. Miraculous things happen in the process of dying. People have epiphanies about the meaning of their lives. They give up grudges they've held for decades. They find dignity despite the most demeaning of conditions.

Sometimes, the things you witness are terrifying. There is a great sadness in watching a person whose last moments are filled with grasping at life, a person who is unwilling to accept his fate and cries out in anger and despair to the very end. Some people die completely alone, and seeing that makes you wonder how something so precious as a life could apparently mean so little to the world. There are many things we don't understand, and the process of dying brings these issues to light for us.

If you are willing to sit with these uncomfortable feelings and to ask difficult questions, you will find many mysteries revealed to you. Your patients will teach you how to appreciate your own life. They will show you what they need to be healed. It isn't always a new treatment or an increase of pain medicine. Sometimes it's just your willingness to face a person full of tubes and oozing sores, and still see beauty. It's a prayer, or a story, or a joke that you share. Whatever it is, if you are present, you will learn. Their lessons are a gift to you. In passing, it becomes a part of your life and your healing.

53. Don't Be Afraid to Cry

A classmate once told me about his experience looking into the gray and sunken eyes of a baby that had been shaken violently. He said it was as if the soul were absent. He thought of the frustration and rage of the person that caused this harm. He thought of the innocence of the infant. Cradling the infant in his arms, he sobbed.

In medicine, we have this idea that we must be impartial and detached to care for patients. This doesn't make sense. To care, we must allow for our own feelings. We shouldn't be afraid to cry. We should be more afraid of the day when we witness suffering and no tears are shed.

Make time to process your grief. Crying is a great catharsis and a sign that you are alive and connected. It may be just a few minutes of heart-felt emotion, like my classmate holding the infant. Or it may entail regular visits to a professional counselor (mental health services are free at most schools). Spend time writing about the experience or talking it over with friends. This time is critical to your emotional well-being and your ability to continue being present with others.

54. Attend the Funeral

One of the most eerie feelings I have ever had was when a patient on our unit died and nobody on the team mentioned it. It wasn't until we didn't stop at his door for morning rounds (as we had routinely done for three weeks) that I realized what happened. It was as if he never existed.

It's not over when the patient dies. Even if we rip up the 3 x 5 card, we have the experience and the memory. We can't pretend it didn't happen.

There is a reason that every culture has rituals surrounding death. These rituals give us closure, allow us to process our feelings, to accept the death, and move on. As doctors, we are not devoid of these needs. We too need rituals that provide closure.

I remember twice finding out months after the fact that patients whom I was close to had died. In both cases, it felt weird that nobody had informed me and that I hadn't gone to the funeral. Families often overlook the medical providers. They, like us, assume that we don't need or have an interest in participating in services after the death.

Sometimes, it may be a good thing to go to the funeral. It brings the life that you knew to a full circle. It allows you to understand that patient as something more than a body that was failing. It may also be soothing to the family for you to be present. Or you can create your own ritual for recognizing the death. I knew one doctor who, every time a patient died, would visit the nursery and hold a newborn child. I recommend that you develop a similar ritual to give you closure.

55. Talk with the Family

Never underestimate the power of the family's contribution in the care of the patient. This includes everyone who is close to the patient, not just blood relatives. Talking with the family will help you to make the best decisions for your patient.

Once I admitted a ninety-year-old Chinese woman who we presumed had a stroke. We weren't sure whether her symptoms were old or new, so we decided to proceed with the work-up for a new stroke. Two days later, I encountered a very upset son at her bedside. He told us that she had been in this condition for many years. She was visiting him from China, had no health insurance, and the bill after two days of hospitalization was $12,000. I felt horrible. Had we gotten the correct history from the family, we could have saved this woman a lot of unnecessary testing and not cost her son his whole life savings.

Families are a rich source of knowledge and support. They can not only help you to understand a patient's disease, but they can shed light on the circumstances that will impact her long-term care. They will help you understand a patient's life: her support network, her living environment, her financial conditions. Sometimes the treatment of a patient requires great life changes—taking extensive medicines, exercising regularly, or a major diet change. Such changes may depend on the aid of the family. If they feel empowered and involved, then the challenges that the patient faces will be that much easier.

56. CREATE PEACE AROUND DEATH

I recently read Sogyal Rinpoche's *The Tibetan Book of Living and Dying*. I was profoundly moved by his plea for doctors to create conditions that allow for a peaceful death. He describes this rite of passage as a fundamental human right—the right to die in peace.

It reminded me of a conversation that I had with one of my medical school classmates, then a third-year student. She described all these very sick people on the neurology service for whom nothing could be done. Yet, every morning they rounded on the patients, posed the latest hypothesis on the disease etiology, and ordered new rounds of lab tests. She said to me, "Sometimes I wonder if it wouldn't be better to transport these people to a sunny rock at the side of the ocean, and let them die." Her reflection struck a profound chord within me that I'll never forget. I had been trained to think of such an attitude as callous, and yet my heart felt some truth in what she was saying.

So many conditions in our hospitals do not allow for a peaceful transition to death. Much of it stems from doctors' inability as doctors to accept death as a natural and necessary part of life. All of the last-minute tests, the attempts at resuscitation, and the extraordinary technology are designed to avoid that inevitable outcome. If we in the medical profession are fearful of death, how can we help our patients to die with acceptance?

Having been at the bedside of a dying patient many times, I believe in what Sogyal Rinpoche is saying: Helping a person to die in peace is the greatest gift of charity you can give. As medical students, you have the time and the influence to make this possible for a patient. You can be an advocate on the team for measures that create greater peace—moving the patient out of ICU when death is inevitable, preventing painful interventions, stopping the pokes and prods on morning rounds. Whatever you can do to create more silence and serenity in the physical environment will have a soothing effect on the patient's state of mind. Give the person privacy and control over as many things as possible. The patient may have beeping monitors and IV tubes attached at all ends, but to preserve the dignity of going to the bathroom alone may still mean a whole lot to that person.

57. WRITE ABOUT A PATIENT

We medical students go through so much hustle and bustle on our daily rounds in the hospital. We pay so much attention to disease and follow so many formulas for treatment. When do we tell—or even think about—the real story of a human being?

Writing creatively about a patient has a deliberate and different intent—to draw your attention to the human side of medicine. When you sit down to write a history and physical, you don't include your feelings and insights. There's no place in medical records for old war stories and lost loves. These are the things of real life, of real doctoring, of real human beings. If you want to stay grounded in that, then occasionally you need to shift your focus and leave behind the medical model.

I remember the first interview I ever did. The patient began by rambling on about the story of his life, about simple joys like taking walks with his wife and going to baseball games. He seemed healthy and vibrant, looking forward to the future. Then he mentioned the reason for his hospitalization, "that little white blood cell thing." At that point, I realized that he had leukemia. He continued talking almost hypnotically, as if discovering for the first time what it feels like to stand at the edge of death.

Afterward, I was so filled with emotion that I felt like the only thing I could do was write. I went to the hospital cafeteria and began filling the pages of my notebook. It helped me to process what I was feeling. Through my writing, I gained a clearer understanding of the gift that he shared with me. I am sure that he has died by now, but on those pages, and in my memory, the man will be with me forever.

58. IN THE FACE OF DEATH, REMEMBER THE POWER OF LOVE

You don't have to be wise and experienced to shepherd someone to the doorways of death. Imagine that you are the person who is dying. How would you react to the loss of everything and everyone you know? What would help you to deal with the loss of control, the feelings of helplessness, the terror of the unknown? The greatest of all healing forces is love, and to be able to give love to another person will awaken deep healing in you as well.

One caution: Forget about what other people think. As a medical student, you may be looked upon as naïve and "soft," or as a novelty because you are still feeling when everyone else has trained themselves to be detached. People who are afraid of being open and vulnerable will also discourage you from doing so. One time, I took a very sick patient for a walk. She had breast cancer with metastasis to her spine. She was in so much pain and was screaming with every step to her wheelchair. The nurses came rushing over to insist that I put her back in bed. She wanted to go, so I continued despite the nurses' disapproval. I rolled her down at the speed of a snail, with her shrieking and groaning at each little bump, so that she could go outside and see the flowers and smell the fresh air. That was one thing she wanted to do before she died.

If we trust first in our hearts, we will be led to the right thing. There's no secret to being with a dying person, above and beyond listening, understanding, and loving. All of these things you have access to long after the drugs and technology stop working. It is your greatest power and the best medicine you may have to offer.

59. LISTEN

One day, a friend of mine got angry with me. He was in the middle of telling a story, and I started to clean the kitchen. He stopped abruptly and asked whether I was listening or not. Insulted, I looked up from my pile of dishes and repeated back the details word for word of what he had said. He looked at me, even more frustrated, and said, "Jen, there's a difference between hearing my words and listening."

Learning to listen is one of the qualities of a great doctor. And yet, when we're thrown on the wards, we're taught ways to get the necessary information from the patient. We are taught how to cut off, redirect, and boil down what the patient is saying. We don't learn how to truly listen. Many times, we get irritated with our patients because they don't give us this information in the way that we want it. Patients that go off on tangents, forget things, or contradict themselves are deemed to be "difficult" patients. If we feel aggravated by our patients, you can imagine how *they* must feel.

One of my professors used to tell me, "If you simply listen to your patients, they will tell you their story." He had a rule that for the first few minutes, he would let the patient speak uninterrupted. For that short time, no matter whether the person was talking about the bump on their toe, or how their dog likes to go to the bathroom, he would simply listen. Often, he said, he would learn more about the patient in those few minutes then he ever could with his own directed questions. For him, it was also a practice in developing patience and compassion for the person. For the patient, it sends a strong message that what they say is important and that someone cares.

When you are able to listen to others, they will share the secrets of their lives. In this, there is such rich beauty, so many lessons, so much pain and joy. These interactions, and the stories that come from them, are what make medical school so meaningful.

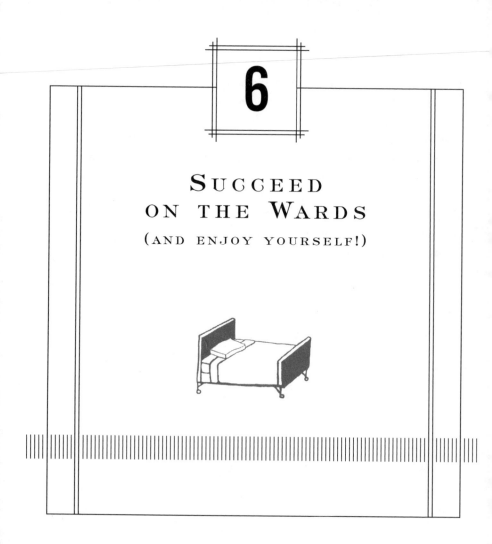

6

SUCCEED
ON THE WARDS
(AND ENJOY YOURSELF!)

60. Give Yourself Plenty of Time for Pre-rounds

Spending sufficient time on "pre-rounds" is essential to your success—and sanity—in the clinical years. As a medical student, you are the first person on the team to see the patient in the morning. During pre-rounds, you review the patient's progress over the evening, examine the patient, and formulate a position on the situation.

How much time you spend in pre-rounds will determine whether you sink or you shine during rounds. It's embarrassing to present a diabetes patient without the latest blood sugar results. You don't have to nail down the differential diagnosis to a tee. It's more important to your team that you take your time, do a thorough exam, and have all the pertinent information.

The problem is that the time for pre-rounds directly competes with one of your greatest needs—sleep. In surgery, when you're rounding at 5 A.M., it's miserable to think of pre-rounding at 3:30 A.M. But I assure you that it's ten times more miserable to be running about chaotic and stressed, just to get an extra half hour of sleep. Go to sleep earlier and don't shave off precious minutes from your pre-rounding time. It's not worth your peace of mind.

If I could do it over again, taking my time is one habit that I would develop with total dedication. During pre-rounds, you can examine patients in a relaxed fashion. You have time to deal with any new events that developed over the night or look for any missing test results. You have time to answer any questions or fears that the patient may have. We need this time to be able to interact with our patients as human beings and not simply be focused on extracting information from them at an ungodly hour.

61. Practice Saying
"I Don't Know"

The average medical student begins the clerkship experience with a lot of insecurity. You want to be the attending, the resident, the intern. You'd even rather be the fourth-year medical student, but you're not. You're the brand spanking new third-year student. You know the least, take the longest, and get in the way the most. This position, albeit somewhat awkward and underappreciated, has one redeeming quality: You're allowed to "not know." In fact, as a third-year student, you're expected not to know anything. Take advantage of this opportunity (while it lasts). Don't cripple yourself or your learning with false pride. Give yourself the freedom of saying "I don't know." What you're really saying is "I want to learn" or "teach me."

I became quite liberal with this response in medical school. Rarely, if ever, did I meet with the scorn that so many of us fear. More often, I found others relieved by my honesty and openness. Residents were more willing to teach. Other medical students were relieved (you mean she doesn't know either?). Patients actually trusted me more. They knew that if I didn't know something, I wouldn't bluff. I would take the time to seek out the necessary information.

This approach is incredibly valuable and quite easy to do. Try it out next time an attending quizzes you on some point of medical trivia (particularly useful with the surgeons). If you're absolutely clueless, just say so. After a while, you will become more comfortable with what you do and do not know. You'll find that you don't have to pretend to be something that you're not. This honesty coupled with a genuine interest in learning is what makes a truly good doctor.

62. Subscribe to Two Medical Journals

Having access to the most up-to-date information in medicine is particularly critical in the clinical years of medical school. In fact, it will be important to you as a physician for the rest of your life. Once you start on the wards, you need to be proactive about your education. Don't wait until you are flooded with articles by your resident that you read either out of guilt or fear. Get in the habit of reading on your own. It is quite common on patient rounds for the attending to refer to the results of the latest randomized control trial on such and such disorder that came out in a major journal. Other attending physicians and residents will be sure to know about it and so should you. This is particularly important if this information will affect clinical decisions regarding the care of your patient. Being in the practice of reading journals ensures that you are in the loop. It also expands your base of knowledge and will allow you to take better care of your patients.

I recommend that you subscribe to one general medicine journal such as the *Journal of the American Medical Association (JAMA)* or the *New England Journal of Medicine.* You should also read one major journal in a specialty field of interest, for example, the *Journal of Bone and Joint Surgery* (for aspiring orthopedic surgeons). Ideally you would start reading journal articles even before you hit the wards. But for most students, this is a bit overwhelming. I recommend that you start your subscriptions when your clinical experience begins. You don't have to read the journals cover to cover. Scan them for articles that pique your interest.

The practice of reading journals is one that you should continue for the rest of your medical career. There's no better time to begin than now.

63. DON'T RUSH

A lot of stress comes from rushing. You bring this stress upon yourself when you try to do too much in too short a period of time. Scurrying about the hospital, you're more apt to lose or forget things. When you rush patient care, you wind up doing a shoddy job and having to repeat your work.

Give yourself more time than you need to complete your tasks. Spend an extra half hour rounding on patients (see #60). Think of it as your cushion time to guard against unpredictable circumstances, or your quiet time when everything goes as planned. Be slow and meticulous when you're drawing blood or doing a procedure. Haste and carelessness can threaten the safety of you and others. Before you leave the hospital at the end of the day, pause for a moment to see if there's anything left to do.

These habits will allow you to be more calm and focused. Almost certainly, you can expect others doctors to be functioning in fast-time, walking, scribbling, and talking at breakneck speed. One day, you may be able to get a history, listen to a patient's lungs, and write patient orders in less than two minutes (hopefully that's not your goal). But as a medical student, to do your best work, take your time.

64. Take a Deep Breath

In medical school, you need techniques to remind yourself what is most important in life. Otherwise, it's easy to get caught up in the minutiae of the day-to-day. Taking a deep breath is perhaps the easiest and most effective way to restore balance when your emotions are off kilter.

This remedy can be used in many situations. If you're taking your Board exam and the room starts to spin, take a deep breath. If an attending in the emergency room yells at you for something, instead of reacting, take a deep breath. Before you give a full presentation to the ICU team, take a deep breath. If a patient withdrawing from heroin is cursing at you while you draw blood, take a deep breath.

This small act has the power to quell fear, diffuse anger, or help you focus on a task. While you're breathing, remind yourself that the immediate situation is very small in the scheme of things. Tell yourself that you have the ability to handle anything. Think calm. Then take another deep breath.

65. Imagine Your Attending
Placing His or Her First IV

This is the rule for every new student on the wards who has just been asked to do something that she has never done before and is scared stiff. Think of your attending placing his first IV. It's hard to imagine a time when a world-famous neurosurgeon had to get help putting on sterile gloves, but we all have to go through this process. It's messy and uncomfortable (for both you and the patient), and it's usually not under ideal circumstances. Yet, it's part of the process of learning.

You need to know that any new procedure will go less than perfectly. I can't tell you how many times I forgot to take off the tourniquet before removing the needle from a blood draw. Blood splattering in your patient's face is less than perfect form. This kind of thing happens, many times in fact, until you learn by experience. The first time I drew an arterial blood gas, we were perplexed by the unusually low carbon dioxide level. It quickly dawned on us that I had poked the patient so many times and caused so much pain that he was hyperventilating, thereby altering his blood gas values! You can imagine my dread in explaining to him why we had to draw another sample.

While the situation is never ideal, it also doesn't need to be horrific. A couple of rules will go a long way. Don't do something that you've never even seen before. That seems obvious, but you'd be surprised how often you will be put in that position ("Don't worry, I'll lead you through it"). We owe our patients some decency, and that means not using them as guinea pigs for our own selfishness or fear of refusing an overzealous resident. Be honest with others about what you have and have not done and your own comfort level. There's nothing worse than being in the middle of placing a femoral line and trying to remember whether the vein is medial or lateral (more than a small detail). Practice the procedure many times in your head before you actually do it on the patient. Make sure that you have all the materials that you need organized in front of you. Always have somebody there who can walk you through it (or at least intervene in the event of a crisis). Finally, don't ever lie to the patient about your experience or level of training. You can conduct a procedure in a confident and compassionate way, without having to pull the wool over someone's eyes.

If you are humble in your learning and honest with others, you will find yourself managing new experiences and responsibilities with grace. For all your mistakes, one day, believe it or not, you will be the attending physician. It's only a matter of time and experience.

66. Learn to Eyeball the Patient

Most of what you learn from a patient takes place in the first three seconds that you see him or her. At this point, you can usually tell whether the person is about to die, in great pain, or mildly ill. Often, a simple glance is enough to diagnose the patient's problem. For example, an elderly patient with a drooping face is likely presenting with a stroke. To be aware of the general picture, what we call "eyeballing the patient," is one of the attributes of a truly seasoned physician.

Once, I admitted a woman with sickle cell crisis. According to the records, she was diagnosed with sickle cell many years ago, and had had numerous medical admissions and surgeries in different hospitals for the disease. She had a shunt in her arm. I started her on the usual for sickle cell crisis—oxygen, pain meds, IV hydration, and so on. The next morning on rounds, my attending came in, took one look at the patient, and walked out of the room. Out in the hall, she smiled knowingly: "Do you believe she has sickle cell disease?" I hadn't even questioned it. But to my attending, one thing didn't fit: she didn't *look* like a sickle cell patient. Sickle cell patients who live till their thirties are generally pale, thin, and worn looking. This woman was plump. A few days later we got the blood smear results: negative. I had become focused too narrowly on her records, and I had forgotten to look at my patient.

When you first meet a patient, take the time to absorb their appearance. Do they look sick? Are they anxious, in pain, afraid? Does anything look particularly odd? The ability to distinguish a critically ill patient from one who is in a lot of pain but generally healthy is a skill of awareness. Often, our medical judgment depends on this.

67. Start a Peripheral Brain

You can't keep it all in your own head, so start a "peripheral brain." This is the jewel box of all medical student's knowledge—the mneumonic for diagnosing a GI bleed, the breakdown of anemia, shortcuts to understanding EKGs. Every clinical pearl that you have learned that you want to drill in your head again and again, you include in the peripheral brain.

Usually, the peripheral brain is a collection of color coded cards on a ring that you carry around with your patient cards. In one section, you may have information on diseases; in another, the structure for examinations (i.e., mental status exam). Whatever you include, make sure you organize it in a way that you can locate the information easily.

Carrying around a peripheral brain allows you to access information in the moment that you need it. If a patient starts to seize, you can quickly flip to the card with the protocol for treatment of seizures. If you have a few minutes while waiting for a seminar to start, review a section of your peripheral brain. Learning is really a matter of repetition; the more you use the peripheral brain, the more you'll retain this information. In time, it will transfer to your real brain.

68. Look for the Elephant, Not Zebras

During the first two years, our learning is academic. To understand the nature of disease, we explore diseases that are obscure, exotic, and unusual. The reality of medicine is quite the opposite. If it looks like strep throat, it's probably strep throat. It's probably not some extraordinary comeback of the bubonic plague.

In medicine, we call the unusual diseases "zebras." When learning medicine, it's more important to recognize the elephant that's directly in front of you than to go hunting down zebras. It's really common sense. If a patient with AIDS gets diarrhea, think first of a common cause for immunocompromised patients. It's unlikely to be a rare parasite that you get in South America. You may have spent months memorizing all of those in parasitology, but you need to alter your thinking when you get on the wards. As one of my professors constantly reminded us, "common things are common."

On the wards, it is better to know the common diseases well, than to know a smattering about everything else. For academic understanding, attending doctors or residents may ask you to reel out an extensive differential diagnosis list. To diagnose and treat the patient, however, you need to pick out the most likely and reasonable problem.

I find this approach the best way to learn medicine. If you have a solid understanding of basic disease processes, you can expand your learning from there. In time, you'll see the zebras, and you'll learn to diagnose and treat them. But in the meanwhile at least you won't miss the elephant.

69. Create a System for the Patient History and Physical

Learning to do the history and physical of a patient is just a matter of creating a recipe and following it. Our brains work better if we follow one system rather than jumping all over the place. This approach will enable you to reproducibly gather the necessary information, organize it, and communicate it effectively.

It doesn't matter what system you use, as long as it works for you. Some like to take the history first, then do a head-to-toe exam (the more common approach for new students). Others start on the physical exam while they're taking the history. If you don't trust your memory, take notes as you examine. I had to let go of one of my favorite techniques—the writing-things-on-the-hand method. After all, ink does not last long when you wash your hands in between every patient.

When examining the patient, always do it in the same order. Use index cards as a reminder, but don't deviate from your pattern. If you ordinarily begin with the ears, don't skip to the chest just because that's the initial complaint. Even if you decide you don't need to look in the ears, at least you go over it in your mind, so you don't forget anything. If you are disciplined in using the same system, you'll always have a complete and thorough exam. It may be awkward at first (as all learning is), but it will soon be second nature.

People will give you advice on different ways to do the history and physical exam. Professors each have their own pet peeves and will often contradict one another. All this pointing in different directions can make your head spin. Be respectful of the opinions of others, but keep the style that works best for you.

70. Let the Patients Guide Your Learning

When you first start on the wards, the amount of information you need to master is overwhelming. Unlike the classroom years, you don't have the structure of daily lectures to guide your learning. *You* decide what you learn.

The best way to learn in the clinical years is from your patients. When you take care of a man with amyotrophic lateral sclerosis, you'll learn everything you need to know about the disease. You'll learn the methods for diagnosis and the standard of care and treatment. You'll read the most recent research articles on experimental drugs. This information directly affects the care you give and may provide new perspectives for the team.

You may find it helpful to organize this information for referral later on. Some of my classmates kept a one-page summary on the disease process for each of their patients. Or you may include this information in your "peripheral brain" (see #67).

Some hospitals have more of one type of patient than another. For example, in my first medicine rotation, I saw more myocardial infarcts than anything else. Other students at different locations saw more HIV patients. If this happens, let the resident know that you want to see a greater diversity of patients. That way, if a new admission comes in that would be a good learning case, he will think of you first.

Learning that is guided by patients tends to be easier and last longer. You may not remember all the reasons for an acute abdomen, but you won't forget the patient who nearly died from ruptured diverticulitis. And you won't forget how he presented in the emergency room. When it's linked to a human being, it's with you for life.

71. Do Small Acts of Kindness for Your Team

Mother Teresa once said that she had never done any great act, only small acts of great love. I thought of this whenever I was struggling with feelings of insignificance on the wards. The hospital is a massive enterprise, with a fast pace and many regulations. Often, it seems like everyone (including yourself) is in survival mode, just doing what it takes to get by.

In this environment, small acts of kindness are like points of light in all directions. It doesn't take much to lighten the day of others. I used to bring muffins and scones to attending rounds to share with my team. The first time I did it, they were surprised and delighted, so whenever I got a chance, I'd bring food. After a while, it became a tradition for us to share food. That one thing did wonders for our morale and our sense of community.

When I look back on my medical school experiences, I am grateful for those little acts of kindness that others showed me. I'll always remember one particular resident, who during a slow Saturday on call, told me to leave the hospital and go to the beach until I was paged (a block away). At that point, I really needed a break. I spent two hours soaking in the sun, jumping in the water, and chasing sand crabs. When he finally paged me, I returned, still with sand in my toes and damp hair, but full of energy and ready to work.

These are the little things, as Mother Teresa says, that you can do for others. It could be as simple as an encouraging word, or time spent truly listening, or a favor you do for another. Do it for the resident that you admire, and do it for the attending doctor that irritates you. Do it when you feel happy, and when you are down or disgruntled. You will be amazed at how your kindness spreads to others. What's more, every time that you act kindly to others, you bring that out more in yourself. Ultimately, the joy that it creates will radiate back to you.

72. Thank People Who Help You

We all want to be appreciated. It's as simple as that. All of our antics for attention, our gripes and groans, they all lead back to this truth. Saying "thank you" is the easiest way of showing your appreciation to those who make your life a little easier—nurses, residents, and doctors. It is also one of the most potent strategies for preserving harmony and good will among people.

Oddly enough, people are often hesitant to show how much they appreciate the help of others. Medical students are worried about being perceived as a "brown nose" on the team. Some may feel vulnerable or embarrassed to admit that they needed help. The truth is, not one of you would be where you are today without the strength and guidance of others. All of the medical knowledge that you gain comes by virtue of the hard work of other people over time.

There is a real power that comes from recognizing how much others give to you. It focuses your mind on the positive, on what is right in your life. You may have the worst day of your life, when everyone—patient and doctor—seems to judge you; still you will find a lab tech who is decent and kind. So recognize that person. What you're really saying is "you make a difference." Often that little "thank you" is enough to keep that person going and encourages him to keep on giving to other people.

After I wrote my first book, I was very tired. I had put so much time and so much of my heart into writing, and I had doubts about whether or not it really made a difference to anyone. For six months, I didn't hear anything, and then I got a letter. It was from a young woman who was thanking me, saying that I helped her overcome her fears of becoming a doctor. She said the book changed her life. When I got a call from my editor asking me to write this book, I was hesitant about the extra work, but I remembered that letter. It was enough to remind me of what I can do, and I accepted.

Be creative in the ways that you say thank you. Sometimes a card is the most practical. But there are other ways. Pick some flowers outside for one of your patients. Write an anonymous note to someone who inspires you. It is those small acts that people remember and will help to ease the way for everyone around you.

73. Ask Others for Advice

You will make a lot of decisions in medical school—like where to go for residency, or even whether to give the patient another bolus of fluid. Remember, in all these decisions you're not alone. Plenty of experienced, caring people are there to help guide you. Reach out to these people for advice.

I've known people who would rather toil in isolation than ask others for help. I've always felt that it's easier and more practical to just ask others for their input. If you're on the right track, you are reassured. If you're working up a patient for an MI that really has a potential GI bleed, a little advice from the intern may save you and the patient a lot of pain. Sometimes, we need another perspective to reach our own conclusions.

When it comes to personal life choices, be selective about who you turn to for help. Seek someone who you feel shares your values, and who will give you healthy and impartial advice. For example, when thinking about pursuing a public service fellowship after medical school, I went to professors who I felt would understand and value this work. Their support in this major decision was crucial for me. It helped me to stand strong in my belief when others dissuaded me.

If you openly seek others' advice, more often than not you'll get what you need. With so many potential sources of help, you shouldn't have to struggle with anything alone. This is a great source of comfort during tough times.

74. Infuse Joy into the Scut Work

Most of what you do on the wards is what we call "scut work." This encompasses anything from running the blood draw down to the laboratory to calling the social worker to getting counseling services for your patient. Some people have an elitist attitude toward scut work. They feel bothered by it, or they feel above it. I've heard many medical students lodge the complaint: "What has this got to do with my education?"

To me, scut work is everything that we need to do to take care of patients. All of it is important. I don't look at the scut work as any more or less valuable than the actual hands-on care. Somebody needs to track down the six volumes of medical records for your patient; why shouldn't it be you? As a medical student, you should think of your role as being an asset to the team in whatever way you can.

Infusing joy into the scut work is the secret to feeling fulfilled on the wards. There is a Zen saying that goes, "When you eat, eat. When you walk, walk." I'd add to this: "When you scut, scut." To approach your tasks in this way simply means to be present and appreciative of every little thing you do. If you look at all your work as valuable, if you appreciate the contribution you are making to the team and patient care, you'll find it easier to enjoy the scut work.

As medical students and doctors, we are here to serve others. The best way that we can do this is to complete our tasks with a light heart. When we do things this way, even the scut work can be joyful.

75. Don't Count on Anything

Don't even think of planning things early in the evening. Or post-call. Or even in the middle of the day. Even if you get out every day by 6 P.M., the one day you promise your girlfriend you'll meet her at 6:30 P.M., all hell breaks loose in the hospital. This is part of your training: accepting uncertainty.

As long as you don't count on anything, you won't be aggravated. Some days, you'll get out while the sun is high in the sky. Other days, you'll wonder why you're still in the hospital at 11 P.M. (and you're not on call!). As a medical student, you are a primary caregiver, and you can't jump ship when you are needed. No matter how much you want to get out of the hospital, your first responsibility is to your patients.

That doesn't mean you need to hang around to accompany your resident to dinner, or other non-urgent matters. If you only dropped in for an hour of surgical observation, you shouldn't wind up holding a retractor for six hours. People will make presumptions about the medical student's time, and you need to advocate for yourself (in other words, don't be a sucker). If you're clear about your priorities, you'll be able to set limits and be flexible when it is truly needed.

76. TEACH OTHERS

One of the best ways to learn is to teach others on your team. You may ask yourself, "What do I know that I can teach?" In fact, you know a lot, and each day you learn more. If you spend a little time to teach, you will find yourself knowing the material even better.

The best teachers I had in med school usually weren't the attending doctors. They were the people closer to my level. In fact, the most devoted teacher I had was the intern on my third-year medicine rotation. Every day, no matter how busy he was, he would hold a teaching session with me. One day, he discussed the basics of EKGs; on another day, we discussed chest pain. He taught me a simplified approach to reading a chest x-ray and coached me through my first ICU presentation. These sessions helped me to rise to the next level and helped him to feel more secure in his knowledge.

The learning curve on the wards is extraordinary. After just a few short months, you'll find that you have gathered numerous clinical pearls. Every time you pass one on, you burn that concept into your brain. Maybe you've learned a clever mneumonic or discovered a great review article. If you make the effort to share this with others, the good results of your learning will quadruple.

After a while, you'll realize that teaching and learning are one and the same. It is a part of the great passing on of knowledge that continues from one generation of doctors to another, and from one team member to another. By playing your part, you help ensure that the spirit of learning is alive and well.

77. Don't Steal the Glory

Many opportunities will be presented for you to try to look smarter than your classmates. For medical students, this presents a real dilemma. To steal the glory is part of our competitive nature. The way of integrity, however, is to allow other people to shine in their own right.

I remember one particular presentation that a student gave on collagen vascular diseases. Upon concluding, the professor asked the student about a cellular receptor type for one of the diseases, surely an obscure fact and a prime opportunity to impress the professor. Before he had a chance to speak, though, another student blurted out the answer, thus devaluing the hard work and learning done by the presenting student.

It is so much easier on everyone if we cooperate rather than compete with one another. Resist the urge to steal the glory on the wards. Make a commitment to answer only the questions posed to you directly, or to a general group. Wait until others decline before you offer up a response. This way, you are assured to leave enough room for others to learn and shine.

Students who genuinely bond with their team, show great effort, and uplift others openly leave a strong impression. Those that trip all over themselves to shout out the name of that new cardiac medication may prove smart, but they also appear as showoffs. It is better to focus your competitive energy on learning as much as you can and on being secure inside of yourself. These students, who show both compassion for others and academic competency, often get the best evaluations.

78. Don't Date Your Intern

I've known more than a few medical students who become enamored of their intern (or resident). You'd be amazed what those late nights on call can do to your hormones. I suggest, however, that you leave the flirting (and anything further) until you are not working together. A romantic fling in the midst of your rotation can unduly complicate your life and that of others.

I can remember one of my classmates who was obviously smitten with the senior resident on my team. As she gave presentations, she would turn rosy and cute, and the two would laugh endlessly at each other's jokes. Not only was this uncomfortable to watch, it was also unfair to the rest of the team. Even if the resident tried to be impartial, he obviously enjoyed her attention and responded to it. When emotions are at play, it's hard to be professional and present for all members of the team. I've also known circumstances that have gone the other way. Unrequited love can have nasty repercussions that aren't pleasant to be around either.

I caution you about where you take seemingly harmless flirting. If you feel strongly about someone on the team, wait a few weeks until you're not working together anymore. That way, your relationship is born out of clarity and not out of a sleepless night.

79. When They Ask for the Two-liner, Give the Two-liner

When giving medical presentations, you need to be succinct. If you can manage this, you'll be a hit with all the residents and attendings, and a great success on the wards. The secret is simple: Give them what they ask for.

The attending doctor or resident will usually let you know whether they want the full presentation or some shorter version (or you'll see it on their face after you begin). A full presentation includes all the details about the patient and can last for up to five minutes. These are the types of presentations that you give for new patients during attending rounds. For medical students, they are a chance to show exactly what you know. The full presentation includes the complete history and physical, describes the subsequent work-up and assessment, and outlines a plan. A two-liner is just that—two lines. This is what you give the resident when you have a half hour to round on ten patients.

You don't want to be the medical student that rambles on. On the other hand, giving a "two-liner" seems impossible to the rookie student. How do you describe an elderly cancer patient who complains of dysuria, gets treated, and then quickly develops a GI bleed and appears to be septic—in two lines? In the first year on the wards, every case may seem as unwieldy. I promise you, however, that in time, you will learn to boil this information down into a few lines that are precise and useful.

Presentation skills are fundamental to your success in the clinical years. Learn to respond to what others need—whether it's the thirty-second presentation or the five-minute version. If you don't know how they want it, then ask.

80. KEEP TRACK OF YOUR STUFF

Figuring out what to do with all your stuff when you first get on the wards is tricky—note cards, clipboards, stethoscopes, books. It doesn't all fit in your pockets. Half the time you're running around at mach speed. It's a setup for loss. Take it from me: I lost my stethoscope so many times, my classmates joked that I should invest in a homing mechanism (instead I tied a string to it and attached it to my jacket).

Looking for a lost belonging in a hospital is an unnerving and usually futile process, particularly if you have been in five different locations on three floors. The losses can be devastating—like your note cards documenting all the lab results, medicines, and critical issues for the ICU patient you need to present in an hour. On top of everything else you have to do, a lost item is enough to push you over the edge.

A few preventive measures will save you a lot of hassle and embarrassment. First, write your name and phone numbers (or pager number) on everything of importance. Second, establish a habit for where you put things. The second time I lost my stethoscope was when one of the attendings on the Ob/Gyn service demanded that we not wear stethoscopes around our necks because it was poor etiquette. It broke my habit; I just couldn't manage to keep that thing in my pocket. Third, only carry what you truly need. There's no sense lugging around all your research articles when you know you're not going to read them in between rounds. It also helps to do a mental check every time you leave a room. I even enlisted one of my patients' assistance. Every time I left, she'd say, "Do you have your note cards?" Finally, take your time. The main reason we lose things is because we're rushing and our minds are in a million places at once.

Forgetfulness is really a matter of awareness. If you take a few easy measures and pay attention to what you are doing, you won't wind up in chaos later.

7

MAINTAIN
INTEGRITY

81. First, Be a Decent
Human Being

In medicine, people tolerate a lot of inappropriate behavior. Take the surgeons. Somehow, because they have long workdays and strenuous conditions, they are allowed to be brusque and insensitive. I don't accept this. Frankly, there are enough examples of compassionate and socially adept surgeons that we need to stop making excuses for the others.

No matter how bad medical school gets, we still have the responsibility for being decent, caring human beings. We are not martyrs forced into this path. Each of us makes a choice to become a doctor, and part of that package is the rigorous training of medical school. We cannot expect those around us to coddle us or to make excuses for us because we're under pressure.

Beware the four cardinal signs of the growing monster within. The number one sign is arrogance. Have you ever felt a slight twinge of delight in a classmate's mistake (it wasn't you!)? Do you feel indignant at your mother's weird theories on heart disease? Are you starting to toot your own horn on rounds? The number two sign is impatience. Do you find yourself interrupting people mid-sentence? Are you running red lights? Do you rush through the H&Ps at the end of the day? The third sign is disconnection. Can you witness great tragedy with little emotion? Do you find yourself avoiding dying patients? Do patients' questions irritate you? The fourth sign is a loss of personal identity. Do you feel more comfortable in a hospital than a park? Have you had an affair with a resident or an attending (worse if they're married)? Do you only talk about medicine?

If you recognize any of these signs, you're already at risk of becoming a monster. Believe me—I've watched classmates transform before my very eyes, and I've felt the beast surge up in me as well. All of us have this capacity. The best way to treat it is to be aware of its possibility and to catch it early. You may need to take some time off, a chance to regain your bearings (see #43). If you're in a rut, get help and take actions to change your situation. If medicine isn't making you happy, then it's best to get out completely.

82. Avoid Pharmaceutical Freebies

Certain things just cross the line. One of these is being a walking billboard for pharmaceutical companies. The buyoff is insidious—lunches provided by Claritin, frisbees courtesy of the latest biotech company, or penlights advertising a new retroviral. The trinkets are tempting, as is everything that's free. But this money comes from somewhere, and it contributes to the cost of our health care system.

This issue is really about determining what you believe in. The culture of medicine is so all-encompassing that you need to take a step back frequently to ask yourself, "Do I believe in this?" This is true whether it be the question of delivering more interventions to keep a patient alive, or standing up in the face of unethical behavior. If we want to be doctors with integrity, we need to build that integrity by making decisions daily that are in accordance with our values and beliefs.

Avoiding pharmaceutical freebies is just one small part of doing this. The larger point is to question why things happen a certain way, whether it's the best way it can be done, and whether or not you want to be a part of it. We are trained as doctors, not as automatons. You are one person that forms part of the complex and dynamic organism that is our health care system. What you think and who you are makes a difference.

It also makes a difference to you. Medicine is so big, sometimes it feels like you're swallowed whole. It may feel like your opinions or actions aren't important. In reality, everything you do matters. If you are living true to your own beliefs, you'll be content. For me, it's pharmaceutical freebies. What is it for you?

83. Beware of Elevator Talk

There's a time and a place for everything. A time to discuss patient cases. An appropriate moment to cry. And time to keep quiet—like when you're riding the elevator. As medical students, we need to remember not to carry our medical conversations into public spaces.

Medical students and doctors can be guilty of being oblivious. We often carry conversations from one space to another without realizing the people surrounding us. To discuss a patient's massive subdural hemorrhage in an elevator is not only not kosher; it's insensitive to patients and their families. For all we know, the daughter of the patient may be standing beside us.

Be mindful of when and where you discuss medical issues pertaining to patients. To us, the hospital is a very different place than it is to the spouse of someone who is critically ill or dying. Our patients deserve confidentiality. And other people are entitled to public spaces that are free of potentially disturbing medical talk.

84. TELL THE TRUTH

It seems like such a simple principle: Tell the truth. And yet, you'll really find yourself tested on this point in the next four years. I don't know a single medical student that doesn't feel, at some point or another, like a fraud. From the time we put on that white coat, we're in the role of pretending to be doctors. But we're not doctors. We're medical students, and we need to accept our place in the scheme of things. We need to stop feeling bad about how little we know.

The best defense for insecurity is the truth. All medical students should know and use this mantra frequently: "I am a medical student. I am doing the best I can. I am learning." Say it out loud. Consider it your greatest responsibility to not confuse this simple point. After all, everyone else will. Residents throw you in over your head, nurses ask you to sign orders you don't even understand, and patients introduce you to their family as "my surgeon." At times, it seems easiest to just go with the flow. But I warn you, pretending you're something that you're not is a slippery slope. It's not just other people you deceive; you confuse yourself as well.

It's a privilege to be a medical student. It's a wonderful position to have, precisely because you don't have to know everything. That's the point—you're learning. So occasionally, patients will grumble about why they have to be poked and prodded by medical students for an hour. And sure, most people would rather have the attending physician place the urine catheter. But it's all part of the process, and if you believe in that, you'll be honest and open at every point. You shouldn't be ashamed that you are only the medical student. You should wear that badge with honor.

85. When All Else Fails, Apologize

There is an old joke about a woman who was complaining to her therapist about all the people who made her life miserable: an irresponsible husband, lazy co-workers, and ungrateful children. The therapist responded, "Okay, bring all those people to me, and I'll treat them. That way, you can get better." Oftentimes, we are so focused on how other people have wronged us that we are unable to look honestly at ourselves. Like this woman, we get stuck in a rut where everyone else is responsible for the bad situation or the frustration in our lives.

In medical school, we need to take responsibility for our actions. In any bad situation, many people have played a part. Rather than gloss over your mistakes, own up to them. A simple apology can work miracles. It smooths over hard feelings and furthers understanding between people.

Medical school is the perfect arena to practice apologizing. You may have a run-in with a classmate or even a patient. And you'll make mistakes. This doesn't have to be the end of the world. If you are in the habit of apologizing, the situation can be nipped in the bud. When your resident is steaming angry because you're late to rounds, or your patient is upset because you discharged him without his medication, you don't have to make excuses. Just say those magic words: "I'm sorry." In time, it will pass.

86. If You Think You Left the Iron On, Go Back to Check

This strategy refers to the experience I had as a child every time we went on a family vacation. As soon as we got on the highway, my mother would say, "Did anyone turn off the iron?" All of us kids would groan and say, "Yes, yes, keep going," but ultimately my dad would turn around and go back. As much as he wanted to, he just couldn't shake that sense of responsibility.

On the wards, as soon as you start taking care of patients, you'll get those nudging feelings, like: "Maybe that was a lump on that prostate" or "Did I remember to put the patient NPO?" Inevitably the thought occurs to you when you're on the way out the door, and you've got a dinner date in an hour. A part of you will say, "Keep going, it's fine," but the conscientious part of you can't let that feeling slip. It nags and nags until you can't stand it anymore.

If you want to be a good doctor, you need to follow up on those nagging feelings. Ninety-nine percent of the time, it's your paranoid mind playing tricks on you, but all you have to do is miss one time, and the house goes up in flames. I used to feel so aggravated by these bothersome feelings, until I decided that this was just part of the territory. If I'm going to be responsible for people's lives, then I need to surrender to that little voice. Now I double-check whenever there's the slightest ambiguity or doubt in my mind.

When you first get on the ward, following up on your gut feelings could be intimidating—even embarrassing. During my medicine rotation, it seemed to me like every patient had pleural rubs. I wasn't experienced enough to know what a real rub sounded like, but I'd still call over my resident, "Could you check this out, I think I hear a rub in the left lower quadrant." It got to be a big joke on my team. Everyone would laugh and humor me, checking out the patient only to find nothing. You can imagine their surprise when one day there really was an unexpected pleural rub!

As a medical student, the best habit you can establish is to follow through with your feelings. It doesn't matter what anyone else thinks, or what little (or big) inconvenience it causes. Tell yourself that the patient is the most important. In the long run, you'll gain the respect of colleagues. You will feel a greater sense of peace. And one day, it could save a patient's life.

87. Stop Looking for Praise

Medical students are considered to be the epitome of success in the eyes of the world. We have good grades and academic awards, the admiration of our peers, and the support of professors. So why are we all so fragile inside? It's because all those years of being lauded by other people has done very little to build up our own sense of self-worth. It has to come from within.

In medical school, people are constantly evaluating you. One person may believe that you're irresponsible and incompetent, and another may think that you're the next Nobel Laureate. What really matters is what you think about yourself. Instead of depending on other people to give you compliments, you need to find ways to recognize yourself.

Here are a few ways to free yourself from praise-dependency. Next time you have a success, don't tell anyone else about it. See how it feels to process that on your own and not need others to congratulate you. Do something kind for another person, and don't take any credit for it. Or the next time you do a project with another person, give them most of the praise.

This approach, if used regularly, will have powerful results. Instead of waiting restlessly for the resident to notice your hard work, you pat yourself on the back. And this time, the good feelings go more than skin deep.

88. Stop Believing That It's Okay to Tolerate Abuse (in Other Words, Stand Up for Yourself!)

In highly stressful situations, there is a lot of frustration that people hold in and periodically unleash on others. In medical school, particularly on the wards, there's no avoiding the sheering forces of abuse. One of the most destructive beliefs held by medical students is that this is normal, to be expected, and hence, tolerated. So when the intern has a bad day, she yells at you. You suck it up, but ultimately it doesn't end with you. It affects your relationships with fellow workers, your spouse, or—heaven forbid—lands you in some explosive traffic brawl (we've all been party to this).

There is an easy way to break this cycle of frustration and mistreatment. It's this simple—do not allow others to mistreat you. Learn to stand up for yourself. Nowhere in the medical school code books does it say that you should tolerate others yelling at you or condescending to you. Some behavior is simply inappropriate.

You know it when it happens. Your feelings are the clearest sign. If you feel disrespected, that's valid enough to bring the matter to the attention of the person. Medical students are often afraid of offending their superiors and getting a poor evaluation as a result. First, *be honest with your feelings* ("Katy, I'm really trying to learn. I know I make mistakes, but when you yell at me, it makes me feel . . ."). Second, *approach the person with understanding* ("Dr. Simon, I understand that you may have been joking, but calling me an 'idiot savant' in front of my patient felt really . . ."). Third, *be tactful;* it's better to pull someone aside in private than address it in a group situation.

I remember one particular person who was very intimidating to me. He was also very moody. We were collaborating on a project, of which he was in charge. Most of the time, we got along great, but other times when he was under stress, he'd raise his voice and start picking apart all the things that I was doing wrong. For a long time, I made excuses for him—he's under stress, he really is a good person. I was afraid of speaking up and jeopardizing our partnership in the project.

In this particular situation, I didn't do him or myself a favor by keeping silent. I realized one day that I was really angry and resentful. This leads to my last point: *Catch it early.* People are often afraid of making a "big deal out of nothing," but it's better to address it in the moment than to hope it goes away and find later you have feelings of resentment. Abuse is a slippery slope; if you tolerate it once, you're sending the message that it's okay to continue this way.

89. Do Not Rely Solely On Your Evaluations

It is important to receive feedback on your progress in medical training. Reading your evaluations, however, can be an anguishing experience for many students and hardly merits the attention we all give to them. To save yourself a lot of grief, don't rely solely on the written evaluation. Seek your own feedback from people directly.

The written evaluation is unfortunately not the best place to learn about one's strengths and weaknesses. It has very little information and is often the product of one person's feelings about you. Depending on your relationship with that person, reading your evaluations is either a big shot in the arm or a big letdown. Either way, it's not a full picture of your work.

It's better to talk with various people you've worked with—interns, nurses, and the attending doctor. The most helpful conversation takes place at mid-point in your rotation. That way, you know how to improve. You should look for feedback again at the end of the rotation. Make sure to keep your own log book of people's comments. This system requires a lot more bravery and discipline on your part, but it will also give you a lot more to work with.

You may choose to read your evaluations at some later point, particularly when selecting your specialty for residency training since the evaluations make up your Dean's letter (the formal synopsis of your performance). Reading your evaluations for this purpose will help you to ensure that nothing is amiss with your choice. It may also serve to validate your ideas about your own strengths. At the very least, you'll have greater perspective on yourself, and you won't rely on the evaluations as your sole source of feedback.

90. Treat Others As You Want to Be Treated

So much of the turmoil we go through in medicine could be eased if we all obeyed this simple rule: Treat others as you want to be treated. In other words, do the right thing.

The strength of the medical team depends on each person supporting and uplifting the other. Small acts of giving can be meaningful, like picking up breakfast for the intern when she's too busy, or taking care of the blood draw for your classmate. Even if you have differences with someone on your team, you can be supportive of that person. Ultimately, your good acts will come back to you.

We should also be careful how much harm we put out in the world. If each of us made a conscious effort to be more gentle, all of our lives would be easier. Try to limit the bad words that you speak about others, even if you're thinking them (including the obnoxious know-it-all classmate). Remember there's never an excuse for disrespecting hospital staff, no matter what their rank, or how frustrated you may be. Be conscious not to boast or brag. What comes easy for you may be quite difficult for another person and bringing attention to this could cause bad feelings (see #77).

8

STAY HEALTHY

91. DON'T EAT HOSPITAL FOOD

To this day, I have never been able to understand how institutions that promote health and healing can serve such greasy-spoon food. With few exceptions, hospital cafeterias are the absolute pits. Iceberg lettuce and goopy Italian dressing, soaked spinach drained of all its nutritional value, potato chips and green jello. The food provided by pharmaceutical companies for noon seminars isn't much better; you can only eat pizza so many times.

If you are truly serious about being healthy in medical school, don't eat the food. You may think I'm kidding, but I see this advice as just as important as everything else you do for your health. If you eat poorly, you will feel poorly. It's really that simple.

We all know there's a strong correlation between our stress levels and our eating habits. I've watched classmates gain forty pounds (no kidding) when they started on the wards. I've seen what I can be driven to when I'm up all night long, when I'm frustrated or bored, or just plain starving. For me, the low point was the midnight meal ritual on the labor unit: a jumbo peanut butter cookie (sometimes two), a plate of curly fries, and a heaping of frozen yogurt—every midnight for three weeks.

Stick to your own healthy eating habits (or develop them). Eat a decent breakfast before you leave the house, and bring snacks with you so you never get to the point where you're driven by hunger to eat substandard food (particularly fatal if all you have is a big jar of candy). Find easy, transportable alternatives that are healthy and contribute to a well-rounded diet. Many of my classmates brought dried soup and heated it up in a microwave. Another classmate would save a portion of her dinner from the night before and eat that. Stick to regular meal times as much as you can, and brush your teeth afterward to discourage snacking in between (I got four cavities in my clinical years).

Eating right sends a message to yourself that you care and that your own well-being matters. If you're healthy, you're better able to care for others. As long as you take proactive measures to eat well, your environment won't determine it for you.

92. TAKE IN LESS CAFFEINE

People who depend on caffeine have a rhythm of energy like a yo-yo. After that first cup of coffee, you're bright and perky. Morning lectures are disproportionately fascinating (a lecture on inner hair cells has you glued to the seat). But by afternoon, you have the attention span of a gnat and everything is horribly dull. If this describes you, beware! You need to kick the caffeine habit.

Caffeine can't sustain you long-term. After a while, it loses its oomph. I remember one late night on the labor unit stumbling down to the cafeteria for a double espresso. Imagine my surprise when I fell asleep at the table immediately after drinking it. I've seen a lot of medical students push their bodies in this way, and they pay for it in the end. If you treat yourself badly, your body will rebel—feeling ragged, getting sick, or depressed.

Believe it or not, you'll have more energy if you give up caffeine entirely. At the very least, try to cut back. After you get over the initial sluggishness, you'll find your natural energy stores rebuilding. Your sleep will be more productive and in tune with your body's needs. After a while, you'll wonder why you liked it so much in the first place.

93. DON'T STAY ANY LONGER THAN NECESSARY

It is not necessary to stay at the hospital one minute longer than you must. A common belief among medical students is that staying late at night will be rewarded with better evaluations. This is like treating an infection with a third-line drug. There are better ways to get honors than lingering after hours. All this accomplishes is that you are exhausted and worn down.

I had the privilege in junior medicine of working alongside one of the most brilliant and compassionate new physicians of our day—my classmate. She impressed me greatly with her knowledge and kindness toward patients. She also stayed late every day. Over the eight grueling weeks, I watched her go from baking banana bread at 5:00 A.M. for morning rounds, to getting illness after illness, to falling asleep in conferences, to finally losing it on our last call night. It taught me a lot. If she had kept consistent and reasonable hours throughout the rotation, she would still have gotten honors. But she could have done it without the illnesses or emotional upset.

The time you spend outside of the hospital is just as important as the workday. Instead of staying late, try reading articles on your patient's disease, or working up the history and physical into comprehensive, compelling presentations. You can't do either of these if you are too tired and burned out from the long hours. If you really want to stay late, do it for the right reasons, like spending an extra moment with your patient. Don't do it to please others.

9

PRACTICE PEACE

94. Don't Speak Negatively about Yourself

I remember one particularly bad call night. I had stayed up all night to research and understand a patient's diagnosis, only to have my ideas shot down by the resident the next morning. That day, I was bombarded by circumstances that were over my head and out of my control. I came home that evening feeling out of sorts, exhausted, and utterly worthless. As so many of us do, I turned these feelings into anger at myself. Conveying the story to my friend Angelina, I must have said the phrase "I am so stupid" a dozen times. She finally stopped me, and made me promise from that day on to never refer to myself in those ways.

You may feel negative, but you don't have to speak negatively about yourself. These words lodge themselves in your consciousness. They affect your mood, your mental clarity, and your interactions with others. In medical school, you can't afford this added negativity in your life.

The first step is to become aware of your speech. Tell yourself that even if you're feeling in the pits, you'll try to speak positively. Even if you don't believe it, say it. After a while, you'll find that the words you speak affect your beliefs about yourself. It's subtle, but it's true. I once heard about research that was done on smiling. The results found that by the simple physical act of smiling, you could induce feelings of happiness. I think that applies to our thoughts and our speech.

Refusing to speak negatively about yourself is an important principle to live by in medical school. It doesn't matter what anyone else thinks. It doesn't matter how badly you goofed. You are a unique, talented, and well-intentioned person. Now speak it.

95. DO NOT TAKE CRITICISM PERSONALLY

Most medical students are already hard on themselves. That's why it's difficult to take any more criticism (we already have enough!). In fact, criticism doesn't have to be as painful as we make it. We need to realize that criticism is part of the territory and stop taking it so personally.

I once had a classmate who was occasionally late. I admired his ability to brush off the opinions and criticism of others. When criticized, he reminded himself that he was a work in progress. He took their words at face value. He interpreted "we think you should be more punctual in the future" as just that. He did not add other meanings like "and therefore we do not like you" or "and we think you are an incompetent student."

When you take criticism personally, you allow all of your insecurities of the past to be triggered by the opinions of someone in the present. It means that an attending who has known you for four weeks can bring up longstanding feelings of incompetency and weaknesses. Learn to distinguish the difference between the two, and realize that most medical professionals are not trained in giving the most sensitive or supportive feedback. Sometimes, you have to decipher the "face value" criticism from the rest of the junk.

96. Forgive People
(Even the Jerks!)

Most of the time, people are nice. But sometimes, particularly on the wards, when stress heats up, social graces go out the window. On a bad day, your attending may snap at you for the smallest of things. It's one thing to be upset in the moment; it's another thing to carry this around for the rest of the day.

To maintain a positive attitude on the wards, practice forgiveness. Tell yourself that every day, you will forgive at least one person—even the jerks. Let go of the idea that someone has to deserve forgiveness, or that they must apologize. No matter how obviously wrong a person is, or how little insight they have into their behavior, you can still forgive them.

On one rotation, the intern assigned to me was downright mean. Every day was a living hell with her, and I dreaded coming in to work. Then one day, she surprised me by talking about herself. She felt miserable—she was unhappy on the wards, she was in a new place without friends, and her husband was cheating on her. I saw a side of her that I had never seen—soft and hurt—and it allowed me to forgive her. If you can put yourself in another person's shoes, it makes it easier to let go of your judgment.

This doesn't mean that you allow yourself to be a pushover, sustaining all sorts of insults and abuse. Those things that compromise your integrity need to be addressed. However, the small things are better to forgive, to let go, and to forget. When you start to look at the world this way, you'll find your own anger and intolerance melting away. And you'll start focusing your mind on the things that really matter.

97. Don't Compare Yourself
to Others

Each of us has a different composite of talents and weaknesses. When we accept this, we'll stop comparing ourselves to others. So it takes you twice as long as others to memorize the bones of the foot. Your strengths may shine when it comes to patient care.

In medical school, there are plenty of opportunities to compare ourselves with others. In small groups and lectures, it's obvious who knows their stuff. People tend to be most vocal when they understand the material (and can make it miserable for the rest of us who are confused). On the wards, for every pimping question that you miss, another student will rattle off the answer. In this environment, every day is a struggle not to feel inadequate.

One defense is to appreciate what you do well—your meticulous history and physicals, good judgment, an ease with patients. Recognizing your strengths makes it easier to accept areas of challenge. Maybe you can't push yourself like others can, or you have children to take care of at night, or you get bad migraines. Then again, these circumstances may give you a valuable perspective that enriches your work as a physician.

Whether choice or inevitability, we need to accept the realities of our lives. As long as we view ourselves as a package, we won't be so focused on the trouble spots.

98. When in Crisis, Look for the Lesson

If you look back on your life, you will probably see that your most important lessons came from situations that, at the time, were less than pleasant. It's true for all of us. Most of us, however, don't appreciate these lessons until after the fact. In the midst of our problems, we see only the pain and negativity.

Without a doubt, you will face difficult times in medical school. You can learn to be more graceful with these difficulties if you pay attention to what that experience is teaching you. Whether it's academic difficulty, relationship problems, or a family crisis, there's a lesson that you can find in the situation. Often, we're so busy simply being upset that we lose the lesson. Or perhaps we feel ashamed about the situation, so we don't want to talk about it with others or face it ourselves.

Looking for the lesson is a powerful tool for personal realization. It allows us to move from self-pity and frustration into a framework of appreciation and acceptance. Try to integrate this tool the next time you have a particular problem. Ask yourself: What is the message that this experience holds for me? What hurts me the most?

If you ask these questions, I guarantee that you will emerge with greater clarity. Rather than simply being angry, you can use your insights to further your growth and understanding.

99. Write Down All Your Negative Thoughts—and Counter Them

Sometimes, we get in a slump. Often we don't know all the reasons we feel low or depressed. It just seems that the world is heavy, and as a result we are too.

The truth is, every slump has a set of thoughts and beliefs that help to sustain it, though they aren't always clear to us at first. One day when I was feeling low, a friend asked me simply, "What is bothering you right now?" To my surprise, I came up with a list of more than twenty negative things floating around my head. It was no wonder I was feeling sad and confused, I was swimming in a sea of negativity!

The truth is that you can change your thoughts. Suppose you fail an exam at school, and you're feeling bad. Your thoughts may be something like this: "I am really stupid," or "Everyone will know about this and look down on me." Once you are aware of these thoughts, you can replace them with more uplifting and truthful statements, such as "I am intelligent and accomplished. I am trying, and eventually, I will succeed," "Nobody is perfect," or "It doesn't matter what anyone thinks." Believe it or not, just coming up with these counter points will make you feel better. Carry this list around with you. Every time you feel a negative belief taking over, repeat in your mind your positive counter point.

Express your positive outlook to other people, even if you don't entirely believe it.

I think you'll be amazed at how a simple shift in thinking can change the way you look at yourself and the world.

100. LET OTHERS LEARN
THEIR OWN LESSONS

On any one day, you may feel frustrated by others. Your significant other is inconsiderate. Your classmate is habitually late. The temptation is to criticize that person in hopes that they will change. Most of the time, however, it's better to let that person learn his or her own lessons.

We expend a lot of energy trying to change other people. I remember a particular aggravation that I kept having again and again with a classmate. I felt like her views on certain issues were narrow-minded, and it drove me crazy. I kept pointing this out to her, until one day she proclaimed, "Jen, you may be right, but maybe I need to learn this on my own." Afterward, I realized how much effort I had poured into showing her all her own errors. I had never stopped to ask whether I was the best person to teach this lesson.

Focusing on others' faults and trying to change them doesn't make us happy. It usually makes other people unhappy as well. So next time you're angry or irritated by someone's actions, practice letting it go.

101. Be Optimistic

In medical school, optimism is essential to your survival. In the hospital, there is tremendous pain and suffering. As students, we have our own difficulties to traverse (like the torture of medical boards). However, if you remain optimistic, even the most awful circumstances can have a powerfully good effect.

In medicine, we try to avoid death and alleviate suffering. But the truth is we cannot *eradicate* death or suffering. Even in this, the destruction of life, illnesses that maim and weaken, we must search for the good. We must learn to see both death and suffering as tools by which to grow. The good of death shows in its unique ability to shock us out of our ruts and schedules and pay attention to ourselves, our loved ones, and our patients. The good of suffering shows those that suffer a level of appreciation for the times of little or no suffering. It allows the rest of us to practice compassion and be grateful for our blessings.

Medical school will give you many opportunities to practice optimism. If you are tired, look forward to being able to rest eventually. If you are grieving, look for the strength you are building and the empathy you can offer to others who grieve. If you are broken, look forward to the day-by-day rebuilding process whereby, like a phoenix, you will soar with greater magnitude. Remember that trials are blessings.

ABOUT THE AUTHOR

Dr. Jennifer Danek is a graduate of the University of California School of Medicine, San Francisco. She is well known and respected in the medical community for her leadership in areas of at-risk youth and violence prevention. As a medical student, she directed and expanded UCSF teaching programs for incarcerated youth and founded Vision Youthz, a non-profit organization to help at-risk and incarcerated teenage boys. For this work, she was awarded the 1996 UCSF Chancellor's Award for Public Service, the Thomas N. Burbridge Award, and the 1998 Martin Luther King, Jr. Award. After graduation, she was selected as an Echoing Green Fellow to expand the Vision Youthz project to a national model for reclaiming at-risk youth.

Dr. Danek is co-author of *Becoming a Physician: A Practical and Creative Guide to Planning a Career in Medicine.* Her unique experience and perspective have helped countless medical students develop themselves holistically in the process of becoming physicians.

Currently, Dr. Danek serves as the executive co-director of Vision Youthz in San Francisco. As a physician, she is committed to addressing the problem of youth violence and bringing the issue to the forefront of public dialogue and the medical community.